Cover Recto

The base image for the recto cover was taken from the public domain. Graphics and photo by Duane R. Chartier. Credit for the base image is as per information below:

*This file is in the **public domain** because it was created by NASA and ESA. NASA Hubble material (and ESA Hubble material prior to 2009) is copyright-free and may be freely used as in the public domain without fee, on the condition that only NASA, STScI, and/or ESA is credited as the source of the material.* **This license does not apply if ESA material created after 2008 or source material from other organizations is in use.**
The material was created for NASA by Space Telescope Science Institute under Contract NAS5-26555, or for ESA by the Hubble European Space Agency Information Centre. Copyright statement at hubblesite.org or 2008 copyright statement at spacetelescope.org. For material created by the European Space Agency on the spacetelescope.org site since 2009, use the {{ESA-Hubble}} tag.

23:12, 15 March 2005 File creation - Bebenko~commonswiki (talk | contribs)

Notes from the Accretion Disk

by

Duane R. Chartier

All Rights Reserved Copyright © 2017 by Duane Chartier

No part of this book may be reproduced or transmitted, downloaded, distributed, reverse engineered, or stored in or introduced into any information storage and retrieval system, in any form or by any means, including photocopying and recording, whether electronic or mechanical, now known or hereinafter invented without permission in writing from the author at drc@authentica.org.

Editorial Assistance / Prodding, admonishing … whatever: Celeste Bryant

Paperback edition   ISBN-10: 0-9706115-0-1   ISBN-13: 978-0-9706115-0-5

Contents

Contents	3
The Author	5
Foreword	6
NOTE 1 - GOING IN CIRCLES	8
NOTE 2 – CIRCULAR SCARS AND OTHER SELF-INFLICTED WOUNDS	10
NOTE 3 – WHY I MUST HAVE CRACKERS WITH MY CHEESE	13
NOTE 4 – A COSMIC REWRITING OF LAMAZE CLASS	15
NOTE 5 – HOW MY DAUGHTER "RILA" GOT HER NAME	17
NOTE 6 – PUSHING A TRUCK FULL OF CHICKENS ACROSS THE US BORDER	20
NOTE 7 – THE GETTY – BILLION BUCK BOONDOGGLE or BULLS**T BAFFLES BRAINS	24
NOTE 8 - ITALY – FELLINI WAS NOT A SURREALIST FILMMAKER	27
NOTE 9 – "WE DON'T DRIVE THAT WAY HERE"	33
NOTE 10 – A FUTURE WIFE TELLS YOU NOT TO BE SO HONEST	35
NOTE 11 – THREE BEST MEN NAMED JOHN	40
NOTE 12 – "MY DADDY WON'T BUY ME A BARBIE!	41
NOTE 13 – "BAMBI …"	43
NOTE 14 – BEN LANDA RENEGADE PH.D.	45
NOTE 15 – "ACID CONSUMES 47 TIMES ITS WEIGHT IN REALITY"	46
NOTE 16 – A MEMORABLE NEWYEARS EVE	48
NOTE 17 – FIRST KEPLER SCIENCE CONFERENCE – CHILDREN IN TOW	50
NOTE 18 – BEING HEALED – 04/20/2016 – OUTSIDE THE LIBRARY	53
NOTE 19 – A MEDICAL MIRACLE	55
NOTE 20 – HOME SCHOOLING	62
NOTE 21 – THE SOLAR CYCLE AND THE PROBLEMS WITH INCOMPLETE RESEARCH	67
NOTE 22 – HOME SCHOOLING – POINTS NEVER MADE … POINTS TAKEN	72
NOTE 23 - FAMILY – CAN'T LIVE WITH THEM … CAN'T KILL 'EM	74
NOTE 24 – DYSFUNCTIONALITY IS THE NEW "NORMAL"	76
NOTE 25 – "LILIAM INTER SPINAS" – ROMANCE ON THE ROCKS	77
NOTE 26 – WHAT THAT GUY NEEDS IS A GOOD RAP ON THE HEAD	84
NOTE 27 – MY BEST BIRTHDAY EVER	89
NOTE 28 – BAIKONUR … SCREW THE RUSSIANS	95

NOTE 29 – ROBERTO AND THE PIRANHA	100
NOTE 30 – INTERNATIONAL TALK LIKE A PIRATE DAY	103
NOTE 31 – WHAT I DON'T GET - BILLION DOLLAR DEAD HAIR	105
NOTE 32 – "IRONIC" HIPSTER	106
NOTE 33 – BREAD AND CIRCUSES	107
NOTE 34 – ART HISTORY CAN CHANGE LIVES	109
NOTE 35 – CLOUDS IN 17th CENTURY DUTCH LANDSCAPE	114
NOTE 36 – PARENTS, A PREGNANT NUN, AND ART HISTORY	119
NOTE 37 – DUANE, "YOU DIDN'T THINK IT THROUGH"	123
NOTE 38 – FENCING FOR A WIFE	127
NOTE 39 – A FLYING HORSE – "END OF THE TRAIL"	133
NOTE 40 – PEOPLE WHO I WOULD LOVE TO BE MORE LIKE – WILSON HURLEY	138
NOTE 41 – THINGS WE WISH WE HAD SAID OR NOT	141
NOTE 42 – THE GYM – A MICROCOSM OF LIFE AND DRAMA	143
CONCLUSION – THERE IS NONE!	149
ACKNOWLEDGEMENTS	150
VERSO COVER	151

The Author

Dr. Duane R. Chartier was an inorganic chemist who entered paintings conservation via degrees in art history and art conservation. He, like most people, has often wondered what the hell he is doing or supposed to be doing. *Ergo … ipso facto*, this book.

His knowledge of fundamentals in materials science and computing led him to the Getty Conservation Institute in Los Angeles, CA, and thence to ICCROM (International Center for the Study of the Preservation and the Restoration of Cultural Property) in Rome, where he coordinated the scientific program. During this time and since then he has practiced as an independent consultant for projects ranging from computer system design at the Peggy Guggenheim Collection in Venice to wall paintings analysis and treatment consultation in the Residenz in Salzburg, Austria.

During his career in art conservation he has moved very large sculptures and installed very large paintings. Some of his more curious dealings have been with the hand and footprints at Mann's Chinese Theatre in Hollywood, CA.

He is currently engaged in a bunch of things that are personally interesting but likely won't earn a single dollar. What he does do to make money is provide the scientific support for authentication of works of art. It was an honor to co-produced (with Roz Roembke) an online catalogue raisonné of the works of Wilson Hurley (www.wilsonhurley.com). In addition, he co-wrote, with the beautiful artist Alyson Souza (www.paintwood.com), *Materials Matter: An Artist's Book of Hours* which is an interesting collaboration between an artist and a materials scientist / art conservator.

Recently he opened a website (www.savant-tools.com) to sell honeycomb panels and cool tools – mostly with the deluded notion that things sell themselves.

Many years ago, he made the bold mistake of starting the non-profit organization, The International Center for Art Intelligence, Inc. (ICAI, Inc.; www.authentica.org). His fondness for oxymorons is clearly illustrated in the name of the organization which, to date, has primarily been a magnet for lunatics.

Foreword

If I am going to send notes to anyone, I should attempt to explaining where and what that place is - **the accretion disk of the Great Existential Black Hole**! The accretion disk is a very thin plane spiraling, spinning faster and faster as the inner edge disappears into the black hole. The accretion disk is where the black hole attracts more matter with its massive gravitational force. It is the zone from which a black hole sucks the matter and energy into itself to power its lustful appetite. There are black holes at the center of almost every galaxy and there are also accretion disks and their existential black holes in most peoples' lives. Zones where actions, thoughts and emotions can easily be sucked into the great black hole and disappear.

We have all been there at one time in our lives – In a place where we can see everything that is spiraling in from the space around and everything that is disappearing into the void ... the other dimension, but we can't do a damn thing about it – it is what it is. Although most people have spent time on the disk of the Existential Black Hole, I contend, in all honesty, most of my life seems to have been spent there. I see it like a badly edited B-movie.

Existential sounds lofty and academic but it is not highly philosophical, it is much more mundane and maybe even common sense. It is basically – things are what they are; things exist; shit happens.

I captured an internet cartoon that was the furthest thing I could imagine from a cartoon. It was the existential GPS that always returned the same location signal to the query of "Where am I?" – "Exactly where you should be!"

"Wholly crap on a cracker!" I have virtually never been where I should be, geographically or metaphysically. I am always perplexed by the silly notations on maps and signs that indicate, with all good intention and confidence, that "You are Here" – well, no I am not, I am here and the here will be going somewhere else ... very shortly.

I have my own existential guru - a very wise woman named Roz who lives on a mountainside. In a recent personal romantic crisis near the black hole edge she cautioned me that "sometimes an abyss is just and abyss." It is very hard to perceive that when you are about to fall in.

The recent incarnation of my life mostly occurs at the gym where I tend to spend more time yakking than I do working out. I lamely justify this by the fact that I have recently ended a twenty-five-year long marriage where I had no real social life outside of my immediate family – all my fault. Having external people to talk to who present even the remotest chance of me being heard is exciting and cleansing. The locker room tends to be a lot like Las Vegas - "What happens in the locker room stays in the locker room." I will only partially violate this credo with three short exchanges.

James (his full identity not given to allow him credible deniability), a very tolerant and affable swimmer, shared a story about his life. He went to a medieval fair and saw some epee fencing. They offered lessons and he was game enough to take a mini lesson (for money, of course, they weren't stupid in the middle ages). After the lesson, he was to have a mock bout but his opponent turned out to be left handed. WOW, instant second lesson required! This struck me so viscerally as how most of my life has been.

Another semi-anonymous compatriot at the gym, AJ, accused me being of a "Triple A" person. My immediate visualization was that of a small battery and I was offended. Then my brain processed the statement and realized that it was a gross mis-typification of my personality type. I quickly assured him that he was way out of line and, at best, I was an AA type. That may explain a great deal.

While doing a group of supersets (pec-flys at that moment) I spotted a new Cybex Cable machine and apparently loudly exclaimed my approval "New Machine" as I raced over to it. Ted, who was working diligently on another machine very calmly said "Squirrel". Probably a very accurate description of my interest in almost everything and my general lack of remorse at be distracted.

NOTE 1 - GOING IN CIRCLES

Most people have been embarrassed more than once in their life but I am willing to stake real money on the fact that very few people have been emasculated ... completely and mortally embarrassed ... by a retired horse.

Yes – true – or as true of any part of my life really seems to me. The scene was intended to be one of manly conquest of a new girlfriend who had consented to go to the Bahamas with me for a quick break from grad school. I decided that it would be a good start to a romantic week to take a beach ride with a few other people that we knew. I personally arranged the ride and the owner asked about everyone's comfort levels and riding abilities. When asked about my own abilities I said that I had ridden quite a bit and horses were usually easy to control. It is likely that this statement was mistake number one for a day that would continue to spiral out of control.

After helping my female friend into the saddle with as much fondling as possible, I was the last one to get on my horse and the group started down the beach. My horse apparently did not want to follow and turned its head to the right and started to circle away from the water and the group who continued down the beach. Initially, I thought I may have been reining the horse to the right so I quickly loosened up and he seemed to be heading in the correct direction down the beach so I just put my heels into him a bit and squeezed. All that happened is he picked up speed, and tightened the circle by turning his head even more extremely to the right. I reined him in, stopped and dismounted. I walked in front and he turned his head straight on to look at me as if there had been no problem. I checked his halter and even the saddle cinch to make sure that there was nothing bothering him – NOTHING.

I remounted and by this time the group was far in the distance. Immediately upon mounting, I urged him strongly on to a gallop to make up the distance. This led to another tight circle to the right so I immediately eased up on the leg pressure and the reins. All this did was slow him down and make the circle considerably bigger. After one more dismount and rather firm words while I held his halter in my hands so he couldn't turn away from the nose-to-nose confrontation, I remounted, continued a partial right turn, and then was confronted by the entire group of riders who we clearly puzzled by what was going on. The owner and leader of the ride then said, as loudly and slowly as possible, as if I couldn't speak English very well, "I thought you said you could ride."

At this point I was not only perplexed but exasperated. I raised my left arm and swung it over the horse's head and said, "It's this f**king horse!". Instantly the horse flinched, turned his head hard down and to the right and I was launched forward and onto my back into the wet sand just as a gentle wave, perfectly sized to wash over me, rolled in. The responses of the entire group were very voluble and my new girlfriend seemed loudest of all. I was completely out of breath from the fall but got up as quickly as possible. The owner dismounted and, without saying a word, switched my horse for my girlfriend's. That switching seemed to do the trick because we both, magically got functioning mounts.

I was completely silent for the balance of the ride amid several tauntings about circular thinking, and circuses (3-ring I assumed). The only thing that persisted in my mind was "A horse, a horse. My kingdom for a horse!"[1] (any horse other than that one!).

When we returned to the holding area off the beach, the owner came over to the uncharacteristically silent me in what I remember to have been an almost scripted line from a bad cowboy movie and with the requisite western accent (that he had not previously exhibited), saying "Well boy… you did say horses were easy to control so I thought you wouldn't have any trouble with a retired polo pony."

This bit of information was centrally important because polo ponies have been trained to turn away from the weight shift of the rider as they swing the mallet. Because I am bilaterally challenged, that was a big problem from the outset. I have limped since I learned to walk so I had never thought much about weighing more on one side than the other until that prone moment in the sand with a timely wave to add insult to the physical and mental injury.

The spiral of negative angular momentum (remember – the accretion disk is spinning in toward the black hole) continued into the evening. After a couple of Cuba Libres, I thought that a night of divine debauchery was ahead. I tried to pull off my t-shirt in the most macho manner possible (whatever that is) and sand was immediately ejected from around the collar. Of course, this brought a round of laughter that turned into a seemingly endless chorus of giggles. There is nothing more erection-destroying than giggles. I really don't mind anyone laughing at me, but it was the timing that I took offense at. There was no grand night of sex and there was never going to be with her because any mention of polo, horses, Nassau, deserts or sand would set off a cascade of giggles. The only consolation I could take from the incident is that my life is quite amusing to others.

---

[1] Shakespeare - **King Richard III:** A horse, a horse! My kingdom for a horse! (_Richard The Third Act 5, scene 4, 7–10_).

NOTE 2 – CIRCULAR SCARS AND OTHER SELF-INFLICTED WOUNDS

I have always subscribed to the notion that self-inflicted wounds don't count. Meaning, very simply, don't expect any sympathy or waste valuable dramatic time on events that you caused. Example, if you light a match to a bridge don't stand under it or, at least, don't expect any sympathy if you do.

In light of the above, I have a very interesting circular scar in the upper quadriceps area of my left leg. Its origin was a sword fight with my younger brother. The swords were wood that I had carefully crafted to give me an advantage in a fight; mine was stronger and broader. That twisted logic was the root of my eventual undoing.

His "blade" was resting on my leg and I decided to slice it in half like Conan the Barbarian or some other mythical, macho movie moron. It broke spectacularly and perfectly except that I had failed to calculate how easily skin and muscle can be penetrated by a sharp stick with significant pressure and velocity. The result was a ten to twelve-inch-long piece of ½" x 3/4" wood driven at least two inches into my quadriceps. It hurt like hell but there was no way I would admit defeat until he was disarmed. I remember enjoying his reaction when I ripped open my pants to see what happened. There was almost no blood but it was very messy. He basically ran away and left me sitting there in my wheelchair with the evidence literally sticking out of my leg. I had just been released from the hospital after about three months of incarceration after an operation on my "bad" leg. There was absolutely no way I was going back to any hospital or any doctor regardless of what it took. I don't remember my age exactly, but I was certainly no more than twelve years old. I was also incredibly determined. It was relatively simple to keep it a secret because there was no way anyone was brave enough to give my mother bad news of any type. According to my siblings, she was apparently worse than "*Ilsa: She Wolf of the SS*"[2].

This is where already living on the accretion disk informed my cognitive processes. It was relatively easy for me to select direct physical pain over dealing with my mother. After retrieving a roll of paper towels and a used grocery bag from the kitchen as well as rubbing alcohol from the bathroom, I retired to the bedroom I shared with two brothers to perform an impromptu surgery. Without any hesitation, I crumpled up several paper towels and grasped them in one hand while I firmly grasped the wooden stake as close to the entrance wound as possible. I remember hesitating and thinking that I needed to have some kind of bit or something to bite down on for the pain, or even better, whiskey! Clearly, I had watched too much TV while in hospital. In very short order I nixed both ideas – I didn't want to hurt my teeth as well as my leg and I didn't like whiskey at all – I had tried several types of alcohol (for experimental purposes only, at least at that point in my life). So instead of the bit I decided that I would pretend to be Tarzan and cover the removal with a guttural jungle scream.

---

[2] "*Ilsa,: She Wolf of the SS*" (1975) http://www.imdb.com/title/tt0071650/. This is a movie in the worst of taste that my bother (of the aforementioned battle) believes my mother to have actually been Ilsa … ANOTHER TALE!

The first attempt at extraction was a complete failure ... I didn't scream, it didn't come out and it hurt even more and started bleeding. I remembered the script and let out a great scream and pulled it out of my leg. Before I could properly react to slap my hand full of paper towel on the copious blood flow, there was a counter-scream from somewhere in the house, "You kids SHUT-UP!"

My brother came in quickly – probably to shut me up. He was upset about the blood but I knew that he was much more upset about the possibility of being implicated. Being the completely sleazy elder brother, I knew I could use that fear to get some help because my plan to just stop the blood was not going very well. Although he did not want to, I more-or-less forced him to go into our mother's bedroom and get a big needle and the strongest thread he could. I told him how to thread it and knot the end. I thought I would never have to admit that one of the many cub-scout proficiency badges that I had received while rotting in hospital was for sewing.

When he realized what I was going to do, he was off faster than a cheap hooker's panties. I grabbed the needle and sewed up the hole with three or four quick punctures that I didn't feel at all. I mopped up a lot of blood and nearly filled the grocery bag. Then I used the alcohol – that was intensely painful! Anyway, it took quite a while to clean things up and to find a way to dispose of the evidence. The trickiest thing was changing my pants in the wheelchair when both of my legs were not doing so well. After a few days, my stitches had scabbed over and I proudly took them out myself.

About a week later I had an appointment to take the cast off my other leg and I had the very unfortunate task of telling my doctor that I had something bothering me in my other thigh. He knew me all too well by this point – he had operated on me three times. He looked at the wound and I knew immediately that any fabrication would be highly unlikely to pass muster with anyone who knew anything. I told him that it was bothering me and that it was very likely that there was a festering "sliver" of wood inside. With a very deft and practiced eye roll at me, he equally deftly probed the area with his finger and got the predictable painful response. He then said that I should tell whoever did the stitches that it was one of the worst jobs he had ever seen. Immediately afterwards he added that it was so bad that even he would not broach it to my mother who always refused to talk to him anyway.

I convinced him to use local anesthetic so that I could watch. He did, and after about five minutes of digging he pulled out at least a one-inch-long hefty piece of wood and turned to me (my face only a few inches away from his) and asked where he might find the sliver. He then proceeded to show me how to properly stich up a wound but said that this one would never be up to scratch because of the original botch-job. I am, to this day, very nervous around doctors but I will never forget his intrinsic sense of humor, that he let me watch, the fact that he did not rat me out to my parents, and his name, Dr. Welply. I hope that the spelling of his name is correct but, in my own defense, I never really knew the correct spelling. He was just the amazing guy who allowed me to save face! Without him things could have gone very badly indeed – he saved me from meeting a definitive problem at the black hole event horizon - my mother.

NOTE 3 – WHY I MUST HAVE CRACKERS WITH MY CHEESE

Most people have endless stories about family, but I only have very few. My only promise is that they are either bizarre or entertaining or both. This is another note regarding my mother, a cat and cat diseases transmitted to humans.

As memory serves, my mother was locally renowned as a terrible cook. The only things I remember that she did well were lemon merengue pie and butter tarts. She would cook things like liver until it became the texture of army boot leather and then she would cover it in an insipid brown gravy and say it was steak. Just the thought of it over 55 year later sends shivers up my spine and starts to upset my stomach.

Cubes of cheddar cheese with a toothpick in them also invoke the same involuntary response in me. Don't get me wrong, I like cheddar cheese, especially a nice aged one. However, it must not be impaled on a stake like one of Vlad the Impaler's criminals. This tale all started with a plate of my mother's ill-founded notion of what *hors d'oeuvres* should be – an array of poorly cut cubes of Kraft cheddar cheese (milk made into yellow rubber) each asymmetrically impaled with a toothpick at random angles and depths.

It was a rare occasion when people came over to dinner and rarer when children were also permitted to eat at the same time. An unfortunate consequence was that you had to eat everything on your plate or, in this case, that you had touched. I had grabbed a toothpick with attached cheese cube and tried to nibble on it but it was awful so I tried to put it down but my mother rounded the corner, looked straight at me, and pronounced "YOU BETTER FINISH IT." At this point the very cute new black kitten (a temporary visitor until another home could be found) was on my lap under the table. The obvious dumping ground for the cheese was the cat in my lap.

The kitten initially smelled it, licked it, took one bite and literally spat it out – to this date I have never seen another cat spit out food. On her very rapid return into the dining room, my mother asked where the cheese was and I completely foolishly lifted it out from under the table and showed it to her. The response was absolutely predictable "Eat that now or you won't get any dinner!" I took a long look at the cheese and a very short one at my mother as she gesticulated that I better get at it. The kitten had licked every part of it but there was no way I was going to tell my mother that I had tried to feed a stray cat her beloved cheese so I took a tiny nibble. That was mistake two – she would not go back into the kitchen until I finished it and I was causing a big problem in delaying her dinner preparations. After eating the cheese, I excused myself from the table without dinner and sent myself to bed for a very unrestful night.

I was only about eight years old, but I had a very distinct feeling that I had contracted some dreaded cat disease and that my days were numbered. The next morning I was up very early and started a somewhat frenzied research campaign in the Encyclopedia. There was a listing for "Feline Diseases" and I looked at a number before finding the one that I was fairly confident the kitten had transmitted to me - **feline pan leukopenia,** also known as cat distemper. It said that kittens were most at risk and that they almost always died (that is clearly why the kitten had no family) and that it was a very contagious viral disease spread through bodily fluid. I checked the symptoms and they included a bunch of things, but I keyed in on depression, loss of appetite and lethargy. I was positive I had it and I really didn't want to die but I was going to do everything that I could possibly do not to tell my mother about my imminent death because of the poor innocent kitten who was also dying. More likely, I was avoiding what would be her furious response to me feeding the cat her precious cheese cube.

After a couple of days of the self-diagnosed depression and lack of appetite, I ventured next door to a very nice woman who was a nurse who often asked me about my stays in hospital. She very quickly understood that I was upset and pried the details out of me. I asked her if pan leukopenia resulted in painful death and she laughed. She then assured me that it was not a disease humans could get. Either she was wicked smart or she had cats (or both). She sensed my incredulity, so she got on the phone to her veterinarian who assured me that I would be alive and well for some time. I am pretty sure that I left him with the impression that I was totally demented.

To this very day (about 55 years) I cannot eat cheese with a toothpick in it or just by itself – I really need a cracker! This incident was a very strong contributor to my desire to become a scientist and be more informed about things that might kill me – that is, if I didn't die first!

NOTE 4 – A COSMIC REWRITING OF LAMAZE CLASS

The worst class of my life was Lamaze class for my first child. I could fill a page with bullet points on why but perhaps I should just write a slightly more comprehensible version of what actually happened. In every way this fits with the title ... it is definitively a story of a swirling disk where the meaning of things and the things become torn apart and if the essential truth of anything actually counted it was sucked into the black hole.

The class was at UCLA and was attended by an assortment of people from university professors (the mother) to professional football players (the father of a different couple). The instructor was a very kindly, soft-spoken woman from the mid-west who had a very large and very poor image of a cat on her shirt. She was so earnest it was always painful for me not to rib her but I was uncharacteristically incredibly restrained.

The simple fact is that I seemed to have somehow been seized by a new personality - quiet, calm, receptive, and supportive. My wife had exactly the same problem but in reverse. She became voluble, uninhibited, and bordered on being so disruptive so as to have both of us ejected. I am absolutely serious – potentially EJECTED. I have been asked to leave classrooms, job interviews and bars but I could never have anticipated being with someone so out of line as to be considered for ejection from a Lamaze class. I swear it wasn't me! She had some kind of hormonally induced mania! Let me recount some of the incidents.

The first class was one dedicated to making everyone feel comfortable with the entire partnering concept of Lamaze and to introduce some of the more fundamental aspects of childbirth like PAIN. I have never asked a woman to get pregnant although I willingly helped when asked. The reason for this is completely selfish. I would never voluntarily extrude a watermelon from any body orifice. Therefore, there is no way I would ask or expect anyone else to. The instructor said that pain would be an issue and she asked the male partners what they would say to their wife as they are accused of causing all of the pain. Pre-empting my more studied and measured response my wife very loudly stated "Shut-up bitch." The response did illicit some very muffled laughter but the look of shock and confusion on the instructor's face was exceptionally clear.

In another class and round of questioning of the males regarding the delivery and child birth a very large and well-muscled black man (whom we later found out was the professional football player) said in a surprisingly diminutive voice, "I really don't think I can take the pain!" His relatively tiny wife, with a very much more powerful voice retorted with "You big sissy!" This created a very good chorus of approving laughs. It was mine turn next and my immediate answer was "I'm very concerned about post-secondary education". It was a bit out of the ordinary but my wife, who normally would have tried to feign that she knew me very rapidly whacked the back of my head. This got even more laughter and I still have no idea why ... the other couple was much more entertaining.

The issue of pain seemed to be quite constant and in response to a question about how pain has been managed historically my wife very quickly blurted out "ALCOHOL", and I am sure she didn't mean rubbing alcohol. This again elicited some laughter from the group but the instructor was completely slack-jawed. Just imagine, fetal-alcohol-syndrome and some very pregnant women balancing martini glasses on their writhing protuberances. WHOA – NOT APRETTY PICTURE!

The incident that almost got us ejected was breathing exercises. The instructor had brought a very questionable visual aid to the exercise. It was a set of postcards with rosebuds. She handed them around and told the men to hold up the cards as their recumbent wives simulated the actual moments of the delivery. The instruction to the women was to envision the rosebud opening! I personally will never look upon another rosebud the same way. What happened was that every time I even started to hold up the card my wife would start giggling and after a few minutes the instructor said that we had to take this seriously, we were disrupting other peoples' concentration and I should stop joking around. I was immensely serious and just tried to get through the class while my giggling wife said not one word to come to my defense.

At least four years later we were having dinner with the only couple in the class who had decided to be caught associating with us. The topic of child birth and Lamaze class came up and **both dinner quests distinctly remembered all of the incidents but had ascribed them to me – not to my criminally responsible wife**. Despite my denials, they were very hesitant to accept that fact that I had not said and done those things because they almost simultaneously avowed that "it is just like you". Finally, my wife admitted guilt and got me off the hook, albeit temporarily.

Perception and habit is often more powerful than truth!

My conclusion is that Lamaze class (at least this particular one) is a cosmic punishment for men who forget to take full birth control precautions at all times or at least to any males who personally revered that moment of conception without weighing all of the consequences.

NOTE 5 – HOW MY DAUGHTER "RILA" GOT HER NAME

This note underlines my laser-like focus on things that mean something to me and my absolute lack of integration of things that might be important to other people. I would like to call it something more sophisticated than being an ass but you can decide for yourself.

My daughter was my first child and the first grandchild for my wife's family. That made the birth very important for her family but the pregnancy had the possibility of being a difficult one so we had to be completely covert until we could get the result of the amniocentesis (about 14 to 16 weeks into the pregnancy). This was relatively easy (except for the silence part!) since we were living in Los Angeles and her parents were in Washington, D.C.

This was a rather tense time but still very positive and anticipatory. Was it a boy or a girl? What would be the name? With the entire uncertainty surrounding actually giving birth the only name I would call the baby in waiting "Basto" (this was my term of endearment for Blastocyst[3]). I should have taken my wife's disapproval of the name more seriously but I have always found it easier to add a stroke of levity to situations that can be rather onerous. Besides, teasing people is one of the very few things that I can say I do well.

My wife was under the care of a Dr. Khalil M. Tabsh, also known as Dr. AMNIO. He was reputed to be the best high risk OB-GYN at UCLA. Apparently, he had an unusually low rate of problems with performing amniocentesis hence ... Dr. Amnio. This was comforting as was his personal directive to start selecting names because he anticipated no problems even though we would have to wait at least one week. As it turned out we had work in Oklahoma City and were sitting in French bistro, with the requisite white paper table cover that you almost never see in France, yet again disagreeing over potential names.

"Penelope" ... no way – my first wife was Penelope – no way in heaven or hell. "Henry" ... right, great idea, the name of a King who happily murdered wives who would not bear him a son. Granted, my name suggestions were no more acceptable but they were not nearly so "normal". I wanted "Zefram" and when she asked where that came from I said, "Star Trek, the inventor of the warp drive!" Needless to say, the name was a no-go.

---

[3] **Blastocyst**: A thin-walled hollow structure in early embryonic development that contains a cluster of cells called the inner cell mass from which the embryo arises. Source: http://www.medicinenet.com/script/main/art.asp?articlekey=18258.

After a couple of glasses of wine and another 50 or so unacceptable names I said, in a most serious way, JACS. "JACS, where is that from?" *"Journal of the American Chemical Society"* where I published one of my first papers.

My wife offered the rebuttal, "That's a boy's name what if it's a girl? I know … RILA". I immediately loved the name and it was the first time that we had apparently agreed upon a name. RILA is an acronym for **R**épertoire **i**nternational de la **l**ittérature de l'**a**rt (the International Journal of the Literature of Art). I expressed my delight that we had made a selection and the elation was very short-lived because I had violated child-naming rules that I was totally unaware of – we could not possibly name our child after a journal! Well, it was back to the black hole for name selection.

After getting the amnio results we knew it was going to be a healthy baby girl. I was relieved to have only half of the naming problem but it turned out to be no less difficult. Months later there was still no resolution.

I will absolutely own the fact that most of the problem was with me. I did not want "used names" or names with personal resonance or names like Virginia where some wiseass (like me) would quip "They called her Virgin for short but not for long."

After 36 very grueling hours of labor a resident came into the room and said that it was my wife's last chance to opt for an epidural. One evil aftereffect of the Lamaze class was to make my wife feel that she was inferior if she could not just squeeze the baby out "naturally" and then go for an invigorating jog. She was exhausted enough to finally be ready to listen to my input when she turned to ask me what I thought. This is an almost verbatim quote; "You know me … better living through chemistry … besides, you are much more macho than I would ever be."

She took the epidural, was asleep in 10 minutes and within 2 hours, extruded a very loud and active baby who could send a stream of pee at least 1 foot into the air after being in the air herself for only about 1 minute. As my wife lay sleeping in her bed I held my daughter in my arms and just kept staring at her. Then a hospital official came in and asked the name. My immediate answer was "Rila … R I L A". It was done, it was official and it seemed cosmically correct. She was unique and she had a suitable appellation.

To this day, I still contend that it was not my direct fault that my wife was unconscious at the time.

Over the years, people have asked me about the meaning or origin of her name and my answers have been highly dependent upon my immediate mood or the number of glasses of old vine zinfandel consumed at dinner. They have ranged from **R**aised **i**n **LA** to **R**eally **i**mpertinent **l**ittle **a**ngel (I am not so sure that I ever actually said "angel"). None-the-less they have always been delivered with the a very high degree of surety and the deepest affection.

NOTE 6 – PUSHING A TRUCK FULL OF CHICKENS ACROSS THE US BORDER

Before being married (a second time) I was living with my girlfriend in Los Angeles. I was in Los Angeles primarily to be with her. She had taken an internship at the Los Angeles County Museum of Art and I had somehow convinced the Getty Conservation Institute that my unique background as a Ph.D. scientist with a Master's degree in Fine Art Conservation was a great asset for them. It probably didn't hurt that I was foreign (albeit Canadian) and had the great French last name - Chartier. One cannot ever underestimate the undue emphasis that non-scientific endeavors put on appearances rather than performance.

I had a J1 research visa (based on being a scientist – not an art conservator). Everything seemed ideal. New girlfriend, good position with an organization with insane amounts of money and questionable management abilities and judgement, a great climate and much potential.

This was the spirit on which we embarked on a planned wild weekend across the border in Mexico. There was no grand plan (pre 9/11, no really dangerous drug cartels, it was 1987), we got in the car and drove to Tijuana and on to Ensenada simply to be on the road and to slake my need for a really genuine fish taco from a street vendor. It was great but I sensed a little trepidation from my partner.

We crossed the Baja Peninsula on Highway 3 north from Ensenada to Tecate. The road crossed through wine country, chaparral and then through incredible boulder-strewn hills. It was so strange that it seemed that after all the acts of creation, God had a handful of bits left and just dropped them here as if no-one would pay attention. It was fantastic and other-worldly.

We cruised into Tecate, a small, sleepy border town. In a misplaced desire for an authentic rather than touristic Mexican experience we decided to just pull up to the first restaurant / cantina to get something to eat. It was early in the afternoon and there was virtually nobody around with the exception of a single person who was seated on the ground and leaning back on a wall. They were draped with a serape and their head was bowed forward and completely covered with a huge sombrero. There was absolutely no movement and my immediate thought was that it was actually a sculpture installed there by the Mexican tourist bureau to add that genuine frontier aura. I had only been in Los Angeles for a couple of months but the entire experience was highly conditioned by Hollywood film shoots and this seemed to be just another cinematic creation.

Driving into town with the air conditioning on had not prepared us for the shock of opening the car doors onto a world that was brutally hot. The air seemed to be thick and provide resistance to even opening the car doors. The temperature was in excess of 110F – blistering and without even the faintest wisp of wind.

Hunger (and a bit of stupidity) propelled us forward through the screen door into the patronless restaurant. Although both of us were poly-lingual, Spanish was not one of them and although Italian may be close it really isn't close enough when ordering food. We manage to gesticulate and order something that definitively had cheese associated with it so my girlfriend thought it was a good idea even though cheese is a particular issue with me.

A few minutes what appeared was a steaming hot bowl full of **LIQUID CHEESE**! Yes, liquid, hot and not on a stick. In fear of losing face I ventured a taste after blowing on my spoon for an inordinately long time – just enough time to make sure that she had taken the first bite and was not convulsing or projectile vomiting. It was terrible and incredibly spicy as well! The only positive thing I could say was that I was intensely happy that the town had a good brewery that made drinkable beer – Tecate. In fact, my lunch was 3 beers and she decided that maybe she should drive to our next destination, Mexicali.

Mexicali is a fairly large border town about half way between Tecate and Yuma, on the California / Arizona border with Mexico. I don't remember much about Mexicali since we were just going to cross back into California and then travel north along the Colorado River (really more a creek this far south).

As we made our way to the check-point we were flagged over to a parking area. Neither of us were in any way concerned as it was very clear that they were checking our car for drugs as we were guided inside into the properly air-conditioned reception area. At this point we were asked for identification and I gave a new California driver's license. This seemed fine but then I was asked my citizenship. I thought that a bit strange but it may have been my accent or the involuntary elongation of out to ooout, as Canadians sometimes do. Of course, I replied proudly and assuredly that I was Canadian. This then brought on the next series of questions.

"Then why do you have a California driver's license?"

"I live in Los Angeles and I have to have a valid license".

"Ah, you live in Los Angeles and is that where you work?" came the next query that was distinctly delivered as if it was a brilliant bit of detective work.

"Yes, it helps to pay the bills, LA is expensive". At this point I got a nudge from my girlfriend and I was trying to figure out what I was actually supposed to do with such a limited amount of information. Did it mean answer less flippantly, answer with a different answer, just say yes, or act as if I had suddenly had been struck dumb or possessed by a foreign language like in a biblical tale? I really had no idea other than she was unhappy with me, the situation, or both.

As I got the nudge another officer came in from outside, leaned over and told our man that the car was cleared. Unfortunately, I then volunteered, "It's no surprise, I haven't used drugs in years." This provoked a very much stronger nudge.

The officer detected my girlfriend's obvious discomfort but it was not with drugs it was clearly with me. He then asked her what her citizenship was … "American" … where she lived … "Los Angeles."

"Would you be living at the same address as the gentleman?" She responded with a long and markedly unenthusiastic "Yeeesss!"

He then turned back to me and asked what my "line of work was". It was probably a bit late but I decided that I should perhaps be a little more serious and definitively less flippant. I said that I was "the new conservation scientist at the Getty Conservation Institute. They just hired me to do a super cool project to develop an infra-red diode laser system to detect trace contaminants in the ambient museum atmosphere!"

My spirited and excited response did not raise an eyebrow or illicit even the slightest comment. He then said "Do you have any more documents?"

I totally misunderstood and told him, "No, I left the research proposal with my boss in LA on Friday but I can send you a copy if you are interested. The lasers are experimental but when they work they are very sensitive – you can probably get down to parts per trillion!"

At this point I did get a response. I got the very distinct impression that he was looking at me as if a were alien. No, not alien, **an alien**. It was clearly associated with me living primarily on the spinning accretion disk.

"Sir, we feel that you may be working in the United States illegally."

"Who is we? I only see you and I am only talking to you?"

"Sir, I requested more documentation such as a visa or work authorization."

"Oh, that ... it's probably in my desk at work." "You could call the Getty Conservation Institute and actually confirm that I work there."

"Sir, we can't do that."

"Why not? Don't your phones work?" This was not a good response but at this point it was incredibly clear that I was dealing with someone who could not see the humor or irony in anything so I figured I had nothing to lose (I received a rib jab instead of a nudge). I then opened my wallet and started taking out all the "documents" I could find and slapped down credit cards, an expired student card, a nuclear laboratory security clearance card from Ontario Hydro (where I had worked until very recently). Finally, I pulled out my new Getty business card ... *Dr. Duane R. Chartier / Senior Conservation Scientist*. He seemed completely unimpressed and remained silent.

As a Canadian I had crossed the US border well over 100 times and never even thought about it. It was 1987 and the worst thing that Canada had ever done was harbor a few people from the Maritimes who periodically clubbed baby seals so I did not understand the problem. The process of getting the job at the Getty was very easy and the J1 visa was all done by their bureaucracy. I received it, put it in my desk and didn't give it a second thought. Now I was confronted by a border guard who only wanted the visa.

My stomach was upset from hot cheese and three beers and I was beginning to lose patience. As my volume began to increase I got a very tight squeeze on my arm and I turned to see what my girlfriend wanted (other than for me to shut up). As I did, the most remarkable scene unfolded in the continuous set of windows looking out onto the road into the US. I stopped whatever I was saying to encompass what I was seeing. The border guard looked up and watched the same scene. There was a completely beat-up pickup truck with string holding down the front hood. In the back was a very tall stack of pretty poorly secured cages full of very loud and unhappy chickens. One cowboy-hatted Mexican was pushing the truck from the driver's side and two others were pushing it from behind over the US border. I turned back to the guard and said quietly but very clearly, "Come ON! Are you kidding me? Are you seriously prepared to prevent a harmless Canadian scientist from doing work on important cultural property but you are personally OK with what is happening on the other side of the glass!"

Perhaps it was my appeal to his personal side but he quickly replied in his most emphatic tone, "Go, just go now, before I change my mind!" I wish that I could say that we beat the chickens into the US but they did have a head start. Clearly some good things do occur on the accretion disk. You just can't predict what, where or when. This may also help explain why I am no longer married to the woman in this note.

NOTE 7 – THE GETTY – BILLION BUCK BOONDOGGLE or BULLS**T BAFFLES BRAINS

How the voyage abroad, to Italy, actually started was an incident at the Getty Conservation Institute that made me realize that I had no future there (a real black hole for me). I had started work on a difficult project to try to measure the actual levels of fumigants (methyl bromide, Vikane – SO_2F_2, and others). This required setting up a clean room and developing infra-red diode lasers to detect very low levels of the gasses in the atmosphere so that realistic experiments could be run to determine what exposure would do to different materials in art works.

This was initially going well until I accepted (like I had a choice!) an invitation to lunch with my boss and the director of research. Of course, I totally misread the situation – I thought that I was the new golden boy and that there was a very high level of interest in the project. Lunch started very well, sake first, a toast to me and my wise decision to work at the Getty, my plans to create an entire Museum Services Department. Then things took an unexpected turn. The director turned to me and very abruptly said, "I need you to work on a project to control the environment for royal mummies at the Cairo museum."

As he started to explain he took out a large red package of Du Maurier cigarettes from his breast pocket and lit one up (possible then – 1987). He said that the Getty had promised to build cases to protect the mummies. He continued on in the usual pompous directorial way telling me how important this was and how good it would be for my career to be involved … yada, yada, yada. While he was pontificating, I took the outside slide of his cigarette pack, opened it up flat and started to draw madly. At this point my immediate boss started to get a bit antsy and leaned over to see what I was doing while pretending to listen.

After I finished my sake and ordered another one I picked up the package and gave it to Frank, my boss. He looked at it very seriously but quizzically and then said, "Duane, this is a serious project!" My immediate reaction was defensive and I replied, "This is very serious".

I grant that my mini-title for the project "Mummy in a Bottle" was seemingly a bit dismissive. At this point the director had stopped talking to himself and wanted to know what was going on. On the package liner I had sketched out my entire case design and rationale. There was a bad drawing of a mummy in a large sealed bottle with the annotations (cramped but still inside the bottle) H_2O (72-78%) and N_2 (1.1 atm). Outside of the bottle there was a little sun symbol and γ (the Greek letter gamma).

I was so proud of myself but that only lasted a few seconds. Frank then said, "What is this?"

"That's my design and rough calculations for the PERFECT SOLUTION." This was the wrong thing to say but it was already being transmitted through the air! Luis, the director, reached over and looked at the diagram and his normally tattooed-on smile began to disappear rapidly. I looked at Frank and realized that I had to make an immediate attempt to save the situation. "I have integrated several things into this approach. My feeling is that the infrastructure in Cairo could not sustain a very high tech approach to the problem. Mummies are complex composite objects that that are very much like furniture so we need to maintain the correct relative humidity but, at the same time, make sure that oxidative processes are minimized and that there is no possibility of aerobic bacterial activity. The external low-level gamma radiation will kill both the aerobes and the anaerobes and the nitrogen at a slight over pressure will insure a stable inert atmosphere. We can do the water by just adding the right amount of ice and the nitrogen by using liquid nitrogen as we evacuate the entire vessel before heat sealing the glass. So the entire thing is self-contained, free of the need of anything but the most rudimentary monitoring, virtually maintenance free, and incredibly cheap. We could probably even get a sponsorship from a milk company because they ship milk in glass-lined tanker trucks – or at least we could use that technology – basically industrial vacuum sealing."

At this point I was again pleased with myself as I had explained the entire rationale faster than I had drawn the solution. Besides, who could possibly be dissatisfied with such an acute and incisive solution? The short answer should have been obvious to me – they were and I really had no idea why. The balance of lunch was rapid and exceptionally quiet. Frank asked me to come to his office where I was lectured about not "handling the director properly". To this day, I have no idea what he meant or was implying and I would rather not know. He then proceeded to tell me that my participation in "the project" was not voluntary and that he had a sample specimen for me. I was more than a bit surprised when he revealed a mummified hawk. Clearly, he and the director had discussed "the project" extensively without any input from the scientist who would be doing it. I did think the hawk was very cool but I told him that there was no need for a specimen or to damage an artifact in any way. The solution I proposed was absolutely sound and more-or-less a no-brainer – besides, I was very busy with a much more important project that would be truly valuable for museums in general.

About a week later Frank called me to his office and said that I had to cover a meeting somewhere (I really do forget because it was trivial) for a few days. When I returned to Los Angeles there was a new staff member for "my project" – a biologist from Spain. It was not a big surprise since, Luis Monreal, the director at that time, was from Barcelona.

I was furious because I had wanted to hire a physicist to work on IR lasers. However, I was mostly furious with myself at being so stupid as to not have anticipated that kind of circus. It should have been obvious that I was a guppy in a shark tank and that real science was never going to be important. Within 24 hours I was having a telephone interview for a senior job at ICCROM in Rome. It was again very clear that PR would always trump real science in an organization founded on "bullshit baffles brains".

Luis Monreal is heavily praised in Getty self-reporting and it was very interesting to me to find a press release on mummies in Marina del Rey[4] about a year after I left. Of course, my solution was unacceptable because it did not integrate, the media, needless technology and a quasi-endless project with vapid photo-ops. Luis Monreal apparently continued his grand plans as the leader of Spain's <u>failed</u> attempt to get the Olympics.

---

[4] September 15, 1987 | RONALD L. SOBLE, Times Staff Writer
Lady X may have been a commoner when she was born about three millennia ago, but no one can say for sure. Her importance, however, far transcends her ancient Egyptian roots and could affect how museums worldwide preserve mankind's culture. Lady X--a mummy--arrived Sunday night at Los Angeles International Airport aboard a passenger jet from Cairo. She was transported in a simple pine, coffin-like box to a laboratory at the Getty Conservation Institute in Marina del Rey.

NOTE 8 - ITALY – FELLINI WAS _NOT_ A SURREALIST FILMMAKER

Before going to Italy to work in what seemed like a dream job that was specifically tailored for my skills my only contact with anything Italian was Federico Fellini movies – bizarre and somewhat surreal. The reason I was going to Italy was basically the same reason I went to live in Los Angeles – to better understand the woman I was living with who was American but grew up in Italy and always got angry preferentially in Italian. Perhaps it was the scientist in me that naively thought that I could do some productive research in this area by observing creatures in their native habitats.

My first day in Italy was the beginning of a two-year long surreal adventure that strongly mimicked the use of hallucinogens. I confess that to this day it is very hard to deconvolute reality from whatever was actually happened on the ground.

I arrived early in the morning (with my girlfriend, Susi) at Fiumicino (Rome's airport) and was, to my absolute surprise, greeted by a diminutive partially uniformed driver with "Dr. Chartier" neatly and boldly printed on a piece of mat-board. I was elated, I was important enough to be picked up from the airport by a limo. The surprises continued as we were escorted not to a limousine but to a high-end BMW. Since I could only guess at the Italian spoken by the driver I was very lucky to have instant translations from my girlfriend (the reason I was there in the first place). He was actually the driver of the director of the organization!

Even in my sleep deprived state I was astounded that such a small organization could afford a BMW and a driver. The incredibly naïve side of me thought that it must have been a donation from a wealthy donor and avid backer of cultural conservation and the arts. He proceeded to take us to the furnished apartment that had been arranged for me in a very nice Deco building on via Anica in Trastevere. Apparently, it was only a few minutes-walk to the office.

Upon arriving at the apartment, we were greeted buy an over-attentive portiere (the female superintendent of the building) who effusively greeted me as Dottore, Professore. I tried to have my girlfriend tell her that it was completely unnecessary and Duane would be fine but it was very clear that the Italian woman was not the only one not listening to me. Our bags magically disappeared upstairs as we were guided to the elevator, with a string of incomprehensible explanations and various episodes of pointing. I think that the woman thought that there were no elevators in the New World and that I may have needed a tutorial. For the first time in my life I felt that I had an entourage. The driver followed us everywhere and once we had "toured" the apartment he told my girlfriend that he would leave and asked what time he should pick me up the next day. It wasn't even 10 am and I was already getting a day off.

I turned to her and told her to ask him to wait 15 minutes while I straightened myself up so he could take me right to the office and I could begin getting oriented. This sparked a good deal of exchange between them and I could tell (mostly by body language) that he was completely taken aback and unprepared for my request. She turned to me and said that he did not think that they were expecting me at the office and that I may be tired and "need my strength". My immediate reaction was quizzical and I asked her if that is exactly what he said. She assured me that it was correct. I was quickly beginning to feel that the entourage was taking over and that if I did not do something incredibly fast I would be following other peoples' agendas rather than my own.

I told her to tell him, as nicely as possible, that I appreciated his concerns but I was determined that I was going to work because that what I was paid to do! She did this and within the next minute he had asked the portiere to use the phone. I cleaned up and he took me quickly over to ICCROM (only about 500 meters away).

The building was impressive and even with the limited amount of research I had done I found that it was the largest 19th century building in Rome. It was right on the Tiber River. Granted, most of it was the Italian Ministry of Culture but my organization, ICCROM, had one end of the four-floor structure and its own central courtyard. As we arrived at the heavy arched front door it was opened by an uncomfortably good looking woman. In almost too perfect English she introduced herself as the Director's secretary and made formal apologies that he could not personally greet me. I shook her hand slowly and proffered my apologies for being a tad overeager to get started and that perhaps the director and I could meet the next day. With no hesitation, she said that would not be possible and she would get back to me on a mutually suitable time. This seemed to be a good sign … smart, tactful, efficient staff.

The secretary took me on a grand tour that included introductions to several of the key personnel. She then took me to my office on the third floor. It was marvelous – ten-foot ceiling, at least 10'x20' deep with large glass doors opening onto via San Michele. She said that she would send in my assistant, Gabriela, as soon as she returned from business at "the ministry" (I assumed the Italian ministry of culture – immediately next door) and that she would brief me and introduce my staff.

I walked to the opened windows, looked down into a courtyard across the street and I could hear female voices singing. It was very eerie and I thought that lack of sleep and jet lag had taken over but as I refocused it was clear that the sound was coming from across the street. I later found out that it was the church and convent of Santa Cecilia. What a grand beginning.

Within thirty minutes there was a firm knock at my opened door. There stood a stunningly beautiful brunette, about 25 or so, who introduced herself by addressing me first, "Doctor, Professor, Chartier; I am Grabriela Krist, your executive assistant." Although I should have been much more attuned to the attractiveness factor I got caught up on the title. Please just call me Duane, I do have a Ph.D. but my mother wanted another kind of doctor. "Yes, professor." The directive and the joke fell on deaf ears.

"No, just Duane. I can't correctly be called a professor if I am no longer teaching in an accredited institution."

"But ... D u a n e. I cannot introduce you as Duane and the staff should not hear me address you in such a manner."

"You mean the staff doesn't think you should use my name?" It was clear that my humor and growing sense of satire were going to be a problem for me or the people around me or both.

After explaining to me basic rules of social propriety she started in with my agenda. WOW! I had all-of-a-sudden graduated to "having my agenda" prepared by some else. Perhaps I was being arrogant and unrefined but I really thought that my agenda should have something to do with what I may think is important. At this point I insisted that she sit down and tell me about herself. She stiffened visibly and took a seat and preceded to tell me that she had worked in a similar capacity for my predecessor. I interrupted her and apologized for my English and repeated that I wanted to know what her background was.

"I am Austrian. My family have been Austrian natives for at least four generations." This response was a bit bizarre but told me a great deal that I already surmised. Teutonic to the core but clearly intent on not being directly linked with any Nazi's (at least by birth). She had an advanced degree in Art History and was very interested in cultural conservation. She spoke, Italian, French, German and English (clearly, but she might have thought that I missed it).

I again quipped that my French was bad and my English was even worse because I had a French-Canadian father and an Austrian mother and the only language that they spoke in common was poor English. This did not even get the slightest smile. My initial impressions of how lucky I was were rapidly disappearing.

She asked when she could bring people into to see me and I told her to go ahead. This seemed to be another problematic directive and she was clearly waiting for more information. I had missed the point entirely. As she stood there silently waiting I suggested that she bring in whoever she could get whenever they were available. I then seemed to set an even more difficult set of requests; "Could I please see the personnel files and CV's of my staff and my program budget for the past five years and the projected budget for the future, say three to four years."

Her answer was exceptionally strange. She said that there were no personnel files that she was aware of on-site and that she was unaware of any budget files and that she had monitored all of the files for some time. I had never worked anywhere where budget was not an issue and not immediately available, usually to be thrown on the desk of some overzealous person who thought money grew on trees. She offered the information that Paolo Pegazzano, the accountant, would know and she was going to introduce him later in the day.

In about ten minutes Gabriela had returned and said that Paolo was doing a very special impromptu lunch for my arrival and that I should go to the staff dining area on the ground floor at about 12:00 – she would be back to accompany me then. She immediately introduced Gael de Guichen who was in charge of Conservation Training in Africa. He was very charming, very French and he was so glib and smiling he made me very nervous. After our initial conversation in French he reverted to English. It could have been my "colonial accent" or a subtler reminder that Africa was indeed divided between English and French. My trepidation was wholly justified because after a few minutes of pointless chatter he said that I could set my mind to rest and that the scientific and technical input to the African programs was trivial and not worth my valuable time – besides, he had it under control. That was that … he was out the door in a flash.

My next visitor came from around the corner – the Library. The ICCROM Library and information system was headed by Marie-Christian Uginet. Her demeanor was very different from her fellow countryman Gael. She was stiff and very formal. She said hello and immediately informed me that she was surprised that I was using Dr. Toracca's office (my predecessor). I thought I had misunderstood her French and said excuse me and asked her to repeat what she had said. She very curtly replied that they had no business getting rid of him and that he would be back. She turned on her heel and very quickly vanished. WOW! I had clearly not done sufficient research or was never intended to know the actual "situation on the ground". It was more than a little chilling to have someone you never met before want you removed from your office before you had been in it for more than three hours. Perhaps my ex-wife knew her and told her things about me that merited such a greeting but even in my depleted condition that was a real long-shot.

At lunch Paolo cooked up an enormous quantity of spaghetti *alla vongole* (with clams) that was delicious and there was plenty of white wine. I met several new people and the general situation seemed to be looking up. This was a very, very different atmosphere than the staff meetings at Ontario Hydro where we would quibble about limited research funding and who had the greatest amount of exposed grey matter and therefore merited more support.

As lunch wound down I tried to talk to Paolo about getting budget information. He assured me that he would get back to me very quickly. Gabriela came over to me and quietly told me what I would be doing for the next couple of hours. The first order of business was to meet the head of public relations for the organization. My mini-briefing included many bits of information including the fact that she was very wealthy, a volunteer and exceptionally well-connected by marriage. All of this information was of a type that I would have never been party to in any previous position that I had been involved with. Not only that, I was more than a bit confused how it would help me do my job as I had presently conceived it.

Within about fifteen minutes a very well appointed and beautiful woman in her mid-forties floated in as if on a breeze. She introduced herself (I don't remember her name) and, before I could rise, she had already sat down on the edge of my desk with her entire right leg showing to the garter belt holding her silk stocking. Holy crap, I had only seen garter belts in porn magazines! It was very hard not to look at it and to attempt to focus on her face. After a few brief answers from me as to how the flight was and how I liked my office she inundated me with people's names and parties that I should be aware of that were coming up and advice on invitations that she would help me with. Parties? I almost never went to parties even if invited. I could not help but think that she was misinformed completely as to who I was and what my real skill set was supposed to be. It certainly did not include schmoozing!

My meeting with the public relations person bordered on a record for me not being able to speak more than three words in a row within a thirty-minute period. As she moved toward the door she turned and stuck out her hand with the palm down. From her references and stories, I knew she was Greek but I was totally unaware of any Greek customs that included an extended arm with the hand down. I grabbed her hand and shook it very vigorously and thanked her for her time. The look on her face was one of disbelief and she left. About a minute later it registered ... I was supposed to kiss her hand ... OMG ... nobody I knew would ever believe me. In fact, it was very hard for me to encompass. Apparently, I had landed in Rome and been transported back a century or more. The alternative interpretation and not a favorable one, is that I totally did not fit in with her social circle and would never be invited to any parties unless her friends had an interest in studying behaviors of indigenous rednecks from the New World.

At this point I was truly exhausted and asked Gabriela to release the driver from his duties of taking me back and that I was quite capable of finding my way. When I got back to the apartment I immediately opened the bottle of champagne that was part of the greeting package and started drinking it directly from the bottle without uttering a single word to my companion – there were no words to describe the flood of disparate thoughts and impressions. I naively thought that a good night's sleep and a few days in the trenches was all that I need to formulate an informed perspective.

The next day was no better as things became stranger but clearer after every question that I had asked. I was informed that the director was in Turkey and would not be back for at least one month. The accountant told me that it would take at least two weeks to get me any budget information. There were no personnel files that I could use or would recognize as personnel files.

I indicated to Gabriela that I needed access to the central computer server. "Do you mean the Wang computer in publications?" was the query from Gabriela. At that point, I did not hesitate to illustrate my complete incredulity by not answering the question at all and just shaking my head in disapproval. It took me about one day to determine that there was no central server, WIFI, or even a proper hardwired network. There were individual desktops (randomly networked) and no laptops that I could detect. It was clear that I had been sent to technological hell for some unknown specific major sin.

After a couple of days of constantly querying everybody that I met on who they were, what they actually did in terms of job description and who made operational budget decisions I was more confused than ever. A long conversation with the director's secretary was very unhelpful and she encourage me not to distract people with so many questions and that the director would be back "soon" to answer any questions such as who was in charge while he was away. Finally, a possibly useful answer ... it was, Jukka Jokilehto an architect whose office was on the fourth floor and whom no one had bothered to introduce.

Arrangisti ("those who arrange things" would be a nice translation) will always win!

Had I not actually experienced these things and not lived in Italy I would have typified them as Felliniesque surreal film making at its most convoluted and strange. Fellini was a documentarian!

NOTE 9 – "WE DON'T DRIVE THAT WAY HERE"

Italy is known for its drivers and that is one of the many reasons I love it so. This is where I really learned to drive. Italians can make three lanes where there are only two and I swear (at least in Rome) that they can park anywhere regardless of whether there is room or not.

Susi (my girlfriend) and I were in the middle of the Tuscan countryside between Siena and Rome. I was driving a Fiat Strada that was acquired from some embassy friends of her parents. It was no sports-car by any means but totally passable to get around in. We were behind a Fiat Cinqa-cento (Fiat 500cc piece of merda!) that was putting along and barely moving. After a few frustrating seconds that seemed like hours I swung around him on a broad long curve in the road that a blind person could see was clear for miles. The Cinqa-cento was just edging past a bicyclist. As I breezed past I saw a uniformed man appear from the low bushes on the roadside.

He stepped onto the road and daringly put out his hand as if that was sufficient to have me come to an immediate stop. I did manage to comply about 300 feet further down the road. I watched my mirror as a clearly irate Carabinieri (Italian State or Military Police) marched up the rocky shoulder. The only things going through my mind at the time were where is his vehicle and what the hell is he doing in the bushes … in the middle of the Tuscan countryside?

The first thing he said when he got to my window was like *déjà vu* but in another language "Do you know how fast you were going?"

"No, but I am sure you will tell me." I managed in my very poor, newly acquired Italian.

Susi, who had grown up in Italy, leaned over me in the car and started to argue with him about whether we were actually speeding and she helpfully added that he shouldn't really listen to me because my Italian was rudimentary and that it was better to talk to her. His response was to silently open my door and gesture me to get out. I sensed that it was probably an innate self-protective response (he most likely had an Italian mother).

"Documenti!" It was pretty clear that he didn't have a radar gun unless he left it in the bushes with the toilet paper so I wasn't too worried about paying or not paying a speeding ticket in a country where I had diplomatic immunity. I pulled out an expired Province of Ontario Health Insurance card and he dutifully copied every single word into his notebook. It was abundantly clear that he did not understand English but what was even more astonishing is that he did not bother looking at the expiration date on the card! I had heard some pretty nasty Carabinieri jokes centering around their pronounced lack of high-level cognitive processes but I had no idea that they might actually be based in fact.

After at least five minutes of meticulous copying he spent at least another five minutes making out a ticket that he asked me to sign. I put an "X" on it and he did not say a word nor did I get a copy of the supposed ticket. One of us was clearly confused.

Susi was agitated and she was more particularly annoyed that when she leaned out my window to try to have a few more words he did not even try to turn to listen. He returned to his cache in the bushes and I got into the car as if nothing had happened. She asked how much the ticket was and when I had to pay it. My answers were, "I have no idea … never." I was still preoccupied with what was so interesting in those bushes but I was destined to never know but left to speculate on the more lewd or crude side.

There were many other incidents such as going through a traffic light in mid-day in Tastevere (Rome) and being stopped by a police man on foot who asked what I thought I was doing. I told him with as much false truth as I could muster. "Il semaforo è rotto (the traffic light is broken)."

He leaned over very close to my face and then pointed back to the light and said "Guarda" (look). The light had just changed.

My immediate retort was "Era rotto (It was broken)!"

He clearly sensed my accent and intonation and said "Non guidare in questo modo qui … non facciamo storie (We don't drive that way here … we don't make up stories)!"

"Veramente (truly)!?" was my response in a tone that bordered on the impertinent.

In a totally exasperated way he dismissed me; "Basta, andare prega (just go please)!" It was the response of a tired policeman who had heard every argument and was just not disposed to engage in one with a flippant foreign smart-ass.

NOTE 10 – A FUTURE WIFE TELLS YOU NOT TO BE SO HONEST

This is another border incident that is emblematic of "not being able to win for losing."

It was 1989. My girlfriend (Susi) and I had been living in Rome for nearly two years. When we returned, we were staying with her parents in Chevy Chase, MD and I was considering a long-term position at the Smithsonian Conservation Analytical Laboratory. The director, Lambertus van Zelst, was a board member of ICCROM (Rome) and offered me an immediate position as a visiting scientist despite the two previous years in what seemed like a war zone. It sounded very good for someone who had just pissed away a permanent job in Rome based on some ill-conceived and definitively not articulated personal morality.

As a scientist, I was not used to "visiting" which implied, to the average person, that I was not actually working on something. I actually had several projects that really interested me but I had no time to work on in Rome when my daily routine seemed to be fighting personnel fires and ominous outbreaks of low IQ that would flow into the computer network.

I very much liked the complete change of circumstances, no staff, no rebellion from anti-technology luddite forces, no dodging potential knife-wounds from the internal Mafiosi. All I had to do was look at things, talk to conservators who were themselves doing research and otherwise try to stay out of trouble. It was an ideal position for me because I was very much going through a brutal self-analysis as to why my life choices were often so incredibly off-the-mark. I left the university to go into the nuclear industry to go back to school to work for the Getty for a few months on to ICCROM for two years then the Smithsonian. Things had indeed changed, I had become much less idealistic, more practical, more cynical, and much less trusting of what people told me – mostly they lie.

Quite rapidly into this new phase of life came a curve ball from out on the accretion disk … my father, who lived in Canada, was apparently very ill and wanted to see me. It is much stranger than it seems because I was fourteen and a half years old when I left home and I was now 37 years old and neither of my parents had previously expressed any desire to contact me. In their defense, I am positive that my demeanor was not very encouraging.

I am totally unclear of my personal reasons for deciding to visit but one factor was that my father's second wife, Della, was a very charming woman who convinced me that it would be a "good thing for everyone". That phrase always sends little shivers up my spine and other parts where the sun doesn't shine because such encounters are rarely good, let alone for everyone. However, she was sweet and clearly loved him so I thought that I should make the gesture at détente if nothing else.

With no plan, I almost immediately got a flight to Winnipeg. I first met Della who retrieved me at the airport and we made light conversation but she kept mentioning things about me that I had not shared with anyone but one of my sisters who had called me about once a year for the past fifteen years just to see how I was. It is unnerving to have a complete stranger know what you have done for a living over many changes.

We went directly to the hospital – really a very bad thing for me. In this case, I admit complete selfishness. Hospitals give me the creeps in a truly visceral way. I had spent much of my youth in them – I hate the smells, the lack of art and beauty, the impending bad news like your roommate is dying – stuff like that. I almost instantly adopt a more flippant attitude than I naturally have and I tend to do at least two really annoying things – I start to talk much too fast and leave little room for anyone else to speak and I make bad jokes about virtually everything. These affectations are intensely annoying to me so I understand completely how other people would feel. It is easy to identify a problem but often intensely difficult to correct it. Before we entered his room, I decided to do my level best to mentally remove myself from the hospital – I was not the patient.

He was indeed not well at all and was in palliative care for a terminal cancer. He was always thin and quite handsome but now he was gaunt and looked very tired. None-the-less he beamed a smile and insisted that I come to him for a hug. There was barely anything to grasp onto and I had to fight very hard not to make an incredibly tasteless joke. I remember most vividly that I had no memory of ever hugging him or of being hugged when I was a child. This only contributed to an entire raft of strange feelings and sensations.

I did not have to ask any questions about his health and he was clearly not in the disposition to provide any information. It was very strange indeed because he kept asking me about my plans and the future. Unfortunately, I allowed myself to backslide a little on the cynicism and I told him, "I have finally learned not to plan very much because the statistics of my predictions are poor". He then totally took me by surprising in stating that he didn't believe me and that everyone knew that I "was brilliant" … really … he said that. I had absolutely nothing to say since I thought my assessment of myself was pretty damn accurate.

After about an hour he was visibly getting tired but he said to Della that he had waited so long for the moment that he refused to go to sleep. I said that I would have to leave anyway because I had to get back to Washington but that I was genuinely glad to have had the opportunity to see him. As we parted he said, "I am so sorry that I was never there for you."

My parting words were, "Thanks, but I probably would not have followed your advice anyway – ask my ex-wife". He smiled.

Della was effusive all the way back to the airport and insisted that I had done something special. The fact of the matter was that I had done something quite selfish – I let myself be understanding and vaguely supportive with no risk to me at all. I could even pretend that I had mended old fences. The only thing I could take away was a slightly greater sense of peace.

At the airport, my calm sense of well-being was soon put to the test. I had to pass through to American Customs and Immigration. The standard questions started:

"Citizenship?"	… "Canadian."
"Your reason for visiting the United States?"	… "I live there."
"Could I please see your visa?"	… "I don't have a visa."
"Sir, you must have a visa."	… "Well, I don't and I didn't know I needed one to live with my girlfriend."
"Sir, you need a visa."	… "Really? I need a visa to live with my girlfriend?"

I won't bother you with the rest of a crazy conversation where I brought up coming to see my dying father, living in Rome, having a UN passport, and truly not understanding what the problem was because the Smithsonian would vouch for me. I felt that I had been sent to a hearing-impaired Customs agent or perhaps he was a relative of the Tin Man from Oz.

After about 30 minutes it was clear that my new home was now Winnipeg (the meteorological asshole of North America). At that point, I had to suppress a real wave of despair powerful enough to propel me through a significant amount of alcohol. I got on the phone. In the first call I explained the situation to Susi and the reaction was not good. I told her that I would call her back because I had to make some other calls. Just before I hung up she did ask if I would be staying with my family. I had not even considered that for one second so my reply was rapid and I simply answered, "No way, I'll get back to you".

After several phone calls and some quick arrangements at the airline desk I was booked on a plane for Toronto. I had called a dean at McMaster University and he said that we could fix up a set of paid guest lectures. Also, the Italo-Canadian mother of a conservation schoolmate, was more than happy to provide haven for a surrogate son to whom she could complain about here actual son who was living in Kingston and not at home where he should be until he was 50. I had also talked to some scientists at Ontario Hydro who would be happy to get me contract work if I would write the contracts. Literally, within two hours, I had lectures, at least one contract and a place to stay with great food and other amenities. Action is always better than despair.

When I phoned Susi to tell her everything she seemed quite upset – something that I had totally missed in the haste to arrange operational details. She wanted to know when I would be back and all kinds of things that I could not possibly do from where I was. We resolved that she would get on the phone the next day to US authorities since my being an alien stranded in Canada might not be a good calling card.

After some considerable soothing, she started to pump me for details of what happened. I very accurately described the situation, the people and the conversations. After some time, we got to the new stuff. Now she was angry at me for being me, **"Duane you absolutely have to learn not to be so honest!"** This was another "holy crap on a cracker" moment even though I did not know the particular phrase at the time. I am pretty sure I have been in trouble for almost everything but I never expected to be admonished for honesty.

Over the next few days Susi worked her magic her way (I dare say without the taint of pristine honesty). She managed to set up a "fiancé visa". Initially I thought she was yanking my chain because, in her eyes, I had been such an idiot. Apparently, it was the very fastest way to get me into the country as long as I stood still long enough to have the ring put through my nose. It took a while to convince me that the visa was real and I still checked it out online after we got off the phone.

I had no real problems with getting married again. We had discussed it when we lived in Italy and I even had the offer of the use of the Peggy Guggenheim Museum in Venice for the wedding and reception. I had done some favors for the director and he said that they would never officially do a wedding so that we could simply call it a meeting or invited seminar (he was not Italian but had clearly been in Italy enough for management technique to rub off). Unfortunately, Susi was the first daughter and her parents did not want a wedding in Italy that would be difficult for the extended family to get to. That was really ironic because I had gone to Italy to better understand Susi who partially grew up there. Whenever she got angry she would revert to Italian, possibly because it was more demonstrative, but it had the opposite effect because it reduced everything to being cute and amusing. It would have been nice to have married there because I would not have been "the fiancé" any longer and it is a fabulous museum full of absolute masterpieces.

I became very comfortable with a surrogate Italian mother – I swear she actually ironed my underwear … really, she ironed my underwear! My nether-regions have never been so well respected. One evening when I went out drinking with some old-school acquaintances and was deposited at some ungodly hour, completely inebriated, she helped me up the stairs to bed! The even more incredible thing was that she did not ever bring up my level of incapacity. The only complaint I could possibly have with Connie was her uncanny ability to emasculate sales people. I went shoe shopping with her and a shoe salesman actually followed her out of the store and more-or-less begged her to consider the shoes for a larger discount. We went back in and I felt I was cast back into Italian surreal street theatre. She eventually decided to pay the thrice reduced price by reaching into her bra to get the money as she continued to exclaim that it was killing her to pay so much!

In addition to my home situation, I loved that I was asked to do a truly interdisciplinary set of talks between the arts and science faculties. As with most things in my life it seemed like a good idea at the time but I fear that the lectures were a totally wasted effort – I had zero apparent effect on anyone. Scratch that, one faculty member in the Art History department totally cemented his hatred for me. That I can take some solace from – he was a complete egomaniac dickhead.

Anyway, I am "stuck" in a very comfortable Canada and my fiancé seems to want me to be bitching and moaning about my terrible plight but that would have been an outrageous lie! I loved my immediate life save for the imposed lack of sex. I lectured on what interested me, they payed me, I had nights out with the boys (something I had very rarely ever done), I had someone who ironed my underwear! Wow, life rarely gets much better than that. In another evening conversation that was full of my appreciation for my temporary situation, my fiancé again suggested that I should modify my approach to being honest with one that was much less transparent.

This interaction and many other parts of my life are completely mystifying to me – how can I be both "completely full of shit" and "too honest"? NO simple answer comes to me immediately and probably never will.

After about 2 months the visa was approved and I very rapidly was committed to be a mail-order groom. We were married in a great location in a small park, Rockwood Manor in Potomac, MD. The wedding was wonderful - small, intimate, with a bride who had a fabulous asymmetric miniskirt and who looked like Judy Jetson. I made that comment to my three best men as we looked down the hall and a canister light illuminated her as if she was about to beam up – totally surreal.

This naturally leads us to another note – Three Best Men Named John.

NOTE 11 – THREE BEST MEN NAMED JOHN

It very difficult not to comment on the consummate lack of imagination that some parents exhibit in naming their children. "John … yep I'll name my kid after a toilet!" "John … I think that is a nice name for him since he will be searching for sex with cheap hookers on random street corners." "John … after the apostle who was a fisherman and was the only one smart enough not to be martyred but probably not smart enough to have written some of the supposed books of the new Testament."

To be completely fair the first two best men were named John and the third was Gianfranco. Well that is probably even worse as a name because it is a compound Italian name Gian (for Giovanni which is JOHN) and Franco (for Francesco). Clearly, his parents were vacillating and couldn't really commit to one name – not a very good start in life or a strong basis for a steadfast character. I also have to be brutally accurate in saying that they were not "best" men at all. I was the one getting married and that undoubtedly made me the BEST man, at least for a limited time.

It was very entertaining for them to all take their best shots at me while I was restrained by the heavy burdens of my new role as husband. They were merciless and I must say that it was warranted give our past interactions. It did take three of them to make their case in public without being eviscerated.

The fact is that they were all unduly tall and unrepenting about their continual need to suck much more air than properly designed persons of modest height. They were also pretty bad squash players if memory serves me well. One of the Johns had to pull down my pants on the squash court to be able to actually score a point. Nothing more to say – all of the rest is just bar talk.

NOTE 12 – "MY DADDY WON'T BUY ME A BARBIE!

Note (#5) was about how my daughter got her name. That dates back to May 4, 1993. This note can be accurately dated to May 19, 1995. Rila was 2 years and 15 days old. How do I know so accurately? Confession – I am a data whore – I always type notes into my computer and often directly into spreadsheets so I can search and sort dates and other items easily.

She was sitting on the edge of my desk and flicking paperclips onto the floor with the obvious intention of getting my attention as I was working on an e-mail. I kept a magnet close by so that picking them up would not be an issue for anyone. Having her on my desk was one of the hidden benefits of working for myself.

I turned to her after about 20 clips hit the floor and asked, "How are you doing?"

"I am very, very busy…Daddy, I need a credit card."

This certainly got my full attention. "Why would you need a credit card?"

There was only a brief pause and then she said, *"**My daddy won't buy me a Barbie**."* This is an accurate quote – third person … accusative (not only a tense but a tone)!

I immediately stopped typing, turned and reached out with a pointed finger to deliver a very pointed speech that I had delivered before … "Barbie is a very poor role model for women, she is commercially produced by evil men at Mattel, anatomically incorrect, too perfect and too thin". My standard approach, but perhaps an unusual lecture for a two-year old, was pre-empted by a small hand that had reached out to touch and rest on my shoulder.

Before I could speak Rila said, "It's okay daddy you don't have to like Barbie".

I had been read, "measured and found wanting". It is particularly disarming when a two-year-old knows how and when to use the third person and even more-so when she seems to know what you are going to say next. Perhaps I was just cleverly baited but, at minimum, I was predictable.

I picked her up off the desk and asked her where we were going to find Barbies and, of course, she immediately directed me to Toys-R-Us. We were there within ten minutes and my only admonition to her in using the credit card was that she could only buy two Barbies and two extra outfits.

Clearly, she had thought about this moment because she immediately selected two Barbies from an entire aisle of them. I don't remember which ones they were even though it took her less than five minutes to do all of her shopping – not a "typical" woman at any age.

Within a few months of the purchase of the first two Barbies, "Ken" was formally invited into the family. He had been a gift of the mother of her best friend (both of who seemed to be waist deep in Barbie paraphernalia). He came decked out in a tuxedo and looked rather natty. Without any ado, Ken was in the bathtub naked. From that point on he remained in the bathroom – for several years – bad hair and naked. Periodically she and her mother would have words regarding his removal but Rila always prevailed.

After one particularly strident attack by my wife upon the general condition (I think the smell) of Ken I stupidly intervened and asked Rila why she didn't take Ken into her room to be with "the girls". Rila's response was unequivocal and strangely existential, "He is where he belongs!"

When I began to recall the event, and write this note I asked her (she is now nearly 24) what year she released the Barbies. The date was definitively July 4 and she texted me "I think I was 8 or 9 for the ritualistic decapitation of my Barbie. I had decided all dolls were conduits of evil." The balance of the dolls was given to a friend but Ken was not amongst them and I choose not to try to imagine the horrors that preceded his demise.

In truth, from the moment I took Rila into my arms, when she was a couple of hours old, I never had much doubt that she was like a cat and would usually land on her feet whatever happened but this particular incident cemented that impression. She knew what she wanted and did not hesitate to state it clearly and concisely – usually without any recourse to discussion. On many occasions in the intervening years she has done some pretty aggressive reverse parenting on me. There is a particularly telling phrase that she has etched in my brain … "Dad… you really didn't think that through!"

NOTE 13 – "BAMBI ..."

Graduate school was a great time at my first *alma mater*, McMaster University (Hamilton, Ontario, Canada). Had it not been for my thesis supervisor, Dr. Ron Gillespie, who doggedly insisted that I stop writing papers for publication and finish my thesis, I would have happily remained a graduate student for my entire life. I loved research, super-acid chemistry, anisotropic superconductors, explosions and the terrified undergraduates that they created.

Another activity that really attracted me was being part of student government. I had been part of a rather politically leftist group that actually managed to form a legal "Union of Graduate Students" at McMaster. There are many interesting anecdotes that resulted from that battle but the note here is really one about a rather tragi-comic failure of editing and probably literacy.

One of the duties I took on with gusto as an executive of the new union was to run a family film festival for graduate students and any interested faculty. We had buckets of money, not from student dues, but from the graduate student bar that paid $1/year rent to the university and sold obscene quantities of alcohol to students and faculty alike. It was almost impossible to spend enough money to remain a non-profit entity. The executive fully funded a baseball league and paid for all equipment. We bought copy machines and offered copies at half the cost of the university's copiers. Another thing that we did that may actually survive a fact check is that we gave about $100,000 to Daniel Ortega[5], the raging socialist leader who later became president of Nicaragua. At the time, he was almost surely on the USA's shit-list. As a student group were proudly a major butt-pain to the university administration.

My notion of the film festival was that young graduate students who had wisely invested in buying drinks in the graduate students' bar should be rebated some of the pittance that they were being paid by the university. The rebate was that we would secure the best films and show them for free so that they could actually afford to take their family. At the time, I had a great interest in having sex but no interest in having a family but I would have had to be a gigantic ass to not recognize that those who had young families had serious financial limitations and needed some support.

Our presentation of *Fantastia* was an incredible success (at the time Disney was very sparing with permissions to show it). Over several weeks of different movies word got out and the auditorium (more than 500 seats) was packed for every showing.

---

[5] Ortega, from 1979 to 1990, was Coordinator of the Junta of National Reconstruction of Nicaragua and later President.

So ... *Bambi* – what could be a better family film? The innocent mother and fawn, evil hunters, chaos, death and transcendence! I went to pick up the films and there were two reels. I thought it was a bit odd but there were often bonus features to lead off the feature. I handed them to the projectionist and went off to relish my new role as social benefactor and staunch supporter of oversexed graduate students who forgot about birth control.

One of the worst evenings in my life unfolded within minutes. What appeared on the screen was a very simplistic black and white graphic - the title "*Bambi meets GODZILLA*"[6]. This was clearly not right and even if I were in my most drug or alcohol muddled state I could not possibly interpret it as anything but potentially very bad. I got out of my seat immediately and rushed toward the projection booth but the damage was already unfolding. As I ran up the stairs listening to the lilting pastoral music I saw a giant reptilian foot totally flatten Bambi whose spindly legs and head were splayed out under the heavily clawed foot of Godzilla. This all took less than 1 minute. It took about 15 seconds for the auditorium to erupt in oohs, screams and very loud cries. I reversed course and made it to a microphone in record time and apologized profusely for the "egregious error" and assured people that the proper reel would be on in a couple of minutes. I have no memory of saying anything in addition to the apology but for weeks afterwards "injured" parents would come into the graduate bar and ask for the "apology beer" (on me, of course).

My report to the Graduate Student Union Executive was very concise. Basically, it read "Bonehead inexcusable error ... execution would not be sufficient." Clearly, they did not exercise the latter option. What really was hard to fathom is that, at the time, I cannot recall that even a single family left the auditorium without seeing the actual Bambi film.

I can't even begin to remember, let alone, quote the string of epithets from irate parents. I am pretty sure some of the comments would have caused Bambi to roll over in his grave. I really got the feeling that some parents would have preferred that it was in my grave.

What I learned from this is **always read the labels at least twice**. Also, Marv Newland's film was really good for the time and when I finally worked up the courage to see it fully, many years later, I loved the credits that read "We gratefully acknowledge the City of Tokyo / for their help in obtaining Godzilla for this film." Maybe I secretly liked the film because it presented tenderized young venison carpaccio - yuummm.

---

[6] This was a student film created by Marv Newland in 1969. The YouTube upload is only 1:32, just about the time it takes to make an incredible mistake. Link: https://www.youtube.com/watch?v=n-wUdetAAlY

NOTE 14 – BEN LANDA RENEGADE PH.D.

Chemists come in all varieties, flavors, and colors. Certainly, Ben Landa, was one of the most colorful that I have ever met. He was doing a postdoctoral fellowship when I was trying to decide what research group I wanted to be in as I entered graduate school. I was a fourth-year chemist and had already been promised a full merit scholarship at my *alma mater* so the only pressure, and not a minor one, was to choose the actual course of my professional life.

Ben and I cemented a tenuous relationship by smoking joints in the walk-in fume hood in the fluorine room. It was a perfect place to smoke dope because nobody in their right mind would really want to be in the fluorine room – molecular fluorine will ignite the atmosphere and consume all of the available oxygen to form OF_2. Besides, there was no odor … dah … walk-in fume hood. By the way, playing with molecular fluorine is really NOT A GOOD THING … if you want to live.

Ben worked for Ron Gillespie, a chemist of some renown, who was one of my target supervisors. Unfortunately, Ben was one of the poorest intelligence sources I could have chosen but there I was. He really did not care what anyone thought and gave the distinct impression that most people couldn't think. Therefore, trying to pump him for any information about the lab or people in it was almost a complete waste of time.

A few years after his finished his Ph.D. I received a postcard with a photo of him standing beside a bigrig cab with this name on the door "Ben Landa, Ph.D.". He was driving his own lumber truck in British Columbia and probably had tapped into the best local sources of weed.

When I started to recall some of the past to relate a fuller account I tried to get in contact with Ben through Linked In. It is probably appropriate that he never even bothered to get back to me. I always had the impression that with Ben it was always full speed ahead … never back. The element that still seem the most incredible to me after so many years is that he seemed to see no real difference between doing chemical research as a Ph.D. chemist or driving a lumber truck. Perhaps that is a very good place to be mentally in a universe that often makes no sense anyway.

NOTE 15 – "ACID CONSUMES 47 TIMES ITS WEIGHT IN REALITY"

As a parent, and an official old fart, it seems necessary for me to state that I do not support the use of drugs ... most drugs ... well ... some drugs like heroin.

However, I went through a period in my late teens when I was prepared to sue a major chemical company, DuPont, for misappropriating my slogan "Better Living Through Chemistry!"[7] As the title of this note would indicate I had a particular appreciation for the power of LSD to modify the normally banal trappings of reality or reduce them to the level of insignificance that most of them deserve. There is little doubt that "Acid consumes 47 times its weight in excess reality".[8]

I make no excuses for using acid almost every day for one year when I was sixteen old. I had lived on my own for almost two years, had to lie continually about my age so that I could work two jobs, and continued to go to school. My decision to leave an abusive home that I had not really grown up in was incredibly easy but the operational problems of dealing with people who I had no interest in speaking to were considerably more difficult – hence acid. I took enough of it so that I could almost legitimately claim that it was a kind of emotional antacid. It allowed me to get through a day without having to talk to virtually anyone. It is highly likely that anyone who paid any attention to me at that time would have assumed me to be mute or, at least, completely socially dysfunctional.

I was surprisingly reasonable and nominally logical for a person who continually hallucinated. It was remarkably easy to distinguish reality from fantasy and imagination when it was absolutely necessary, such as when people would feel that it was their prerogative to enter into my personal space. What I wish to talk about is a particular event that lead me to believe that although acid was a wonderful thing there were some potentially damaging or unpredictable consequences to its habitual use.

On a damp weekend morning, I decided to hitch-hike into Toronto from Hamilton to avoid any incidents that might occur from dropping three hits of window pane for breakfast. I was going to see a girlfriend who really did not want me driving my motorcycle while I was stoned (I clearly chose her and had to thumb). I was a bit dismayed because I did not seem to be feeling any effect at all.

---

[7] Better Things for Better Living...Through Chemistry." Was the actual slogan that DuPont adopted it in 1935 and it was their slogan until 1982 when the "Through Chemistry" was dropped. "Better Living Through Chemistry" was a variant of the phase that was well known.
[8] "Rolaids consumes 47 times its weight in excess stomach acid" was the advertising phrase originally used to sell the antacid and I have no idea where the transcription to LSD and reality consumption occurred - perhaps it was me when I was stoned ... who knows.

A very brightly colored Cadillac pulled over and I ran up and quickly opened the door. The acid had clearly been working because I was completely taken aback (a very unusual thing for me at that time). The interior of the car was enormous ... the size of a hockey arena! I felt that I would have to shout so that the driver could hear me but, logic prevailed as I had to convince myself that the car was a normal size in ambient reality. I quietly got over my preemptive thank you and then realized that my normal discriminatory cues for reality versus hallucination had all but disappeared.

The driver was wearing a very much larger than average cowboy hat. There was a 6-pack of beer on the central consul of the car that was precisely the correct size for a 6-pack. He asked me if I wanted a beer and I politely declined because I never drank beer before 9 am. He then offered me a cigarette. I did not really smoke but I accepted it to be polite. Everything was fine until he reached over to light it. The cigarette seemed very long as it protruded from my mouth and I worried that I might have a problem once he lit it. As he touched the car lighter to the end it burst into savage flames that seemed to need a 3" fire hose to put out. I tried to remain very calm but I moved my fingers as close to my mouth as possible so that they would not be seared by the flames. As I took the first puff smoke rose from the tip in a series of symbols that I thought might be Apache or Navaho smoke signals ... but for what?

After a few more tentative puffs I rolled down the window and ejected the cigarette. I was transfixed by the trees as we passed them. They all seemed to be touching each other and passing along the wind. When I looked forward I could not help let out a gasp that I could not suppress. The driver immediately asked if I was alright. I assured him that I was fine but that I had never driven that fast before. He asked me again, this time more seriously and insistently, if I was alright. I looked at the speedometer and we were only going about 70 mph. I told him that I needed a minute to check.

What I saw through the windshield was an incredible foreshortening of everything ... it was all compressed and coming at me much faster than 70 mph ... more like 3000 mph. I looked out of the car to my right side and the trees and buildings were all normal and passing at about the speed on the speedometer. I then looked back over my shoulder to see a world that had been stretched as if it had been drawn on a balloon that someone had blown up far too much. My reality filters failed.

I immediately turned to the driver and kept saying ... Did you see that? Did you see that? He very quickly pulled off at the next ramp and told me that he had forgotten something and had to turn around. I got out and thanked him as he drove off and did not turn around at all.

What he failed to see and understand is that I SAW, FELT AND HEARD THE DOPPLER EFFECT! It was fantastic and may be one of the contributing factors into my decision to become a scientist. He may have needed therapy due to our interaction but what can you say about a guy in a cowboy hat who drinks beer before 9 am?

NOTE 16 – A MEMORABLE NEWYEARS EVE

This note is the only New Year's Eve that I can remember. It is consistent with my life and my general contention that people usually remember extremes not the norm.

It was December 31, 1999 and we were preparing to have a dinner party to usher in the new year. It had been a busy Christmas and I had just finished assembling a new white desk (from IKEA) for my six-year-old daughter, Rila. She was now set up with a new desk and a new computer to replace my old laptop that she had been using for a couple of years.

My son, Raef who would be four in the coming April was doing his usual thing … marauding. Long before even the previous the Christmas holidays he had found a very effective way to escape the house. He could very easily get through the dog door and make the prison break into a large back yard. It was okay since the yard was fenced but I had argued unsuccessfully to my wife that we could get an electric dog collar just in case he tried to make a more complete run for it by tunneling out or something of that nature. The first time we found him outside was when he was about two years old. After a frantic search, we found him calmly sitting in an empty wooden wine box and guzzling the dregs of a bottle of wine … REALLY!

While I was finishing up work on the desk his first target was the garage which was not a garage at all but a cross between a workshop and a high-end hardware store. Leaving the garage door open was certainly not wise but I had not yet integrated his abilities at hunting and seeking. He had obviously been observing me work and decided that he liked the Makita cordless drill. What could be better than a tool that looked like a gun and made cool noises too! Thankfully, his drilling tests were only on the outside wall of the garage but I removed the weapon. He was too small to frisk and I really did not want to risk finding any other contraband.

I went back to preparing something else and within ten minutes I heard an accusative cry with my name in it from the kitchen. I ran in to find that Raef, the burrowing boy, had proceeded to remove products from under the kitchen sink. I had mistakenly decided to rid the place of all the "child-proof" latches that are really "adult-proof" latches (at least for some). It was made abundantly clear to me that my son's randomization of the sink area was a direct result of my poor judgement.

I proceeded to clean the area up and made the further mistake of not Velcro-ing him in place. Within four or five minutes my daughter let out a piercing scream from her room where Raef was trying out his new ideas of Abstract Expressionism with a black Sharpie on Rila's white desk.

This resulted in me sending them both away with her as overseer so that I could use solvent and hopefully get high enough myself to forget the last hour or so!

One would think that this was enough but somehow my daughter forgot her task and I went into the living room to see him stuffing something into the floppy drive on a computer. At this point I gave in and personally intervened in order to tire him out as much as possible or at least to reduce the level of destructive energy.

After chasing him around on the floor as if I was the dog (the dog, by the way, was too lazy to bother) I decided that I was sufficiently tired and I would lay back on the bed with him between my legs. That is when the real spiral into the black hole began!

As I prepared to lay back and watch something on TV with him what I saw coming at my face at blinding speed was the back of my son's head. He hit me perfectly in the middle of my face. There was a very loud scream (this time from me). Instantly I had him in my hands, stood up and rethought tossing him as far as I could, but I did launch him into the center of the bed. My nose had made a cracking sound loud enough to be heard in the kitchen. Both my wife and daughter came in as I rushed into the bathroom trying to contain a handful of blood that had belatedly gushed from my nose. They stood at the door as if they were an attention-starved audience and then both made horrified noises regarding the remodeling of my face. At this point, I turned to the mirror and had to do a double-take as I did not recognize myself. My nose was smashed and on the left half of my face.

Having been in hospital too many times I realized that I would have to spend New Year's Eve in an emergency waiting room with a raft of wailing people with all kinds of alcohol-induced self-inflicted wounds. I decided to "samurai-up" and steeled myself to do instantly what would take the hospital hours. I grabbed my floppy nose, clinched my teeth and forced the cartilage back into place with a Tarzan-like shriek of relief. I must have done something right because the blood flow stopped and I was acutely aware of being able to use both nostrils. One of the two spectators winced but I have no idea which one. I silently went back to the bed and lay down with my t-shirt front covered in blood. Someone said that perhaps I should not lie on the bed with a bloody shirt and my only response was a wave of my finger in a particularly dismissive manner.

Frozen peas are a great icepack if you have something that hurts like hell, is protruding much more than normal (no ... not what you may be thinking ... nose ... this is about my nose) and had been bleeding copiously. As I lay on the bed with a pounding headache and a rapidly freezing nasal area my wife contributed the lovely gem "Peace on earth and peas on Duane!" This was certainly a day that I will never forget. A very positive thing that I can report from the incident is that I had almost no swelling or bruising and my nose was probably better than the one I had previously. On New Years Day, a cosmic thank you was sent out to the Jolly Green Giant.

NOTE 17 – FIRST KEPLER SCIENCE CONFERENCE – CHILDREN IN TOW

All parents try to steer (manipulate and/or bully) their children into agreeing with them or at least into sharing a set morals or even interests. This is one of the benefits of having an essentially totalitarian power of someone. It also helps if you do not have a particularly well developed conscience.

On December 5-9, 2011, the 1st Kepler Conference was held at the NASA Ames Research Centre at Moffet Field in California. If I had not communicated my incredibly strong interest in exoplanet (planets around other stars) research and intelligent life elsewhere in the universe than I was really a poor communicator. I had to make a few phone calls but I managed to make sure that my children and I had a place at a history making conference. Somehow, I even managed to book us rooms for an exceptional rate right on site. Having said this, I must reveal that they were definitively the only children there (Rila was just 18 and Raef was 15).

The Kepler spacecraft (launched March 7, 2009) was amazingly successful in detecting planets around nearby stars by looking at the changes in the light curves for the stars as the planets transited their suns[9]. A set of about 160,000 stars in the constellation of Cygnus just above the plane of the Milky Way was chosen as the target area. The results of the brief functional period of the probe are astounding[10]:

Confirmed Planets: 2330

Planet Candidates: 4706

Eclipsing Binary Stars: 2165

We are now in a very different galaxy and universe than we were in even 20 years ago when there were virtually no exoplanets known. This very tiny patch of our backyard in the galaxy is teeming with planetary systems; some of which have planets in the habitable zones of their stars. We are highly likely not to be alone in this vastness. Statistics demands that there are other sentient beings in the universe. The only sad thing is that there seem to be few or none in Washington, D.C.

The first conference was a very big event internationally and it was attended by some of the youngest, keenest and most motivating scientists. This was my nominal goal - to show my kids that all scientists weren't boring, staid and unidimensional. To be brutally honest, at least half of my effort was completely self-serving. If I had another life this was one of the things I would be doing for a living.

---

[9] The original Kepler spacecraft mission was reformulated when it could no longer accurately point at one fixed spot (May 11, 2013).

[10] These numbers are from the NASA website (http://kepler.nasa.gov/Mission/) as of March 31, 2017. The numbers have been rising as the data analyses continue to be done.

Were the presentations above the heads of my children? NO – comprehension of all materials often comes at many levels and very often must come with multiple exposures over time. Each day we would end with a kind of mini question and answer period or a wild blind speculation session over dinner. One of our most spirited and perhaps most dispiriting discussions centered on the startling differences between the Hollywood presentation of E.T. and the naked scientific realities of living in a vast universe. I made very clear that I had always believed that there had to be intelligent life all over the universe but we would likely never speak to any of our neighbors – even the nearest stars to earth distant when scaled to the speed of light are immensely far when scaled to our capability to travel in space.

It was marvelous to be able to show them the forces and the clear passions that propel science and that are often hidden from the general view of the public. With the enthusiasm of the newly reported exoplanet discoveries and some within the "habitable zone" I was cast in the role of bringing my kids crashing back to earth by saying that although I had always believed that the universe was rife with intelligent life that it was highly unlikely that we would ever be able to communicate. The nearest neighboring stars with any planets in the habitable zone are many light years away. As a scientist, I am bound by some simple principles – the inverse square law being a very important one. What would it take for us to establish first contact with other intelligent beings? The power requirements alone for any decipherable communication at light year distances are huge (in the order 1000th or more of a star's own power). The signal to noise ratio is critical and stars are somewhat noisy and cranky celestial characters. Even in the most speculative science fiction few civilizations have harnessed stellar level power for communications.

In the public's eyes astrobiology is really looking for E.T. and that's O.K. We are all, in our own imaginations, torn between the unlikely event of contacting intelligent life and the scientific difficulties in defining and recognizing the signs and marks of life even on this planet. Keeping an open mind is really very important.

So where does that leave us – exactly where we have always been – seeking to understand our origins and those of the universe – trying to understand the miracle of life on this planet and on others if possible. Even more clearly, we must look at our own solar system most thoroughly for the biological answers we seek. The immediate challenges are already being addressed – Curiosity on Mars. Enceladus is the likely next candidate given the changing emphasis in the Cassini mission.

I think that the biggest thing that I wanted from the conference was to make my children realize that I see them wherever they can envision themselves. Until I started writing these notes I had not considered this material to be relevant to me living on an accretion disk but the truth is that my entire approach to dealing with my own children has been, at minimum, somewhat extra-terrestrial compared to most of the parents whom I have met. In fact, some of them though I was pretentious and arrogant and tried to "show my kids off" as if they were some kind of new clothes or something. My only intention, ever, was to treat them with respect and make them understand that they had valuable things to give to the world. For many years, I considered this conference adventure self-serving and a bit of a bust. To collect a different opinion, I texted both of them with the following message:

> "Memories, reaction, comments when I say Kepler.
>
> I need background data. Thanks, D"

My son Raef had much more to say than he usually does:

> "I remember the conference and getting to meet all the scientists actually involved and what they did Planetary discovery and how cool that was
>
> Discovery of new and amazing abundance of different star systems and how they function."

I immediately texted him back:

> "Did you feel like you belonged?"

His reply made me feel as if I had not been a completely selfish ass.

> "Yes. Although I didn't always understand everything it didn't matter for the conference, it was a place where people shared things, not just their research and it never felt that what I had to say was any less important."

This response was texted to me on May 26, 2016. I had no idea that the experience was more than I could have hoped for – I had written off the conference as a bust and had, for years, had to accept my self-criticism of my level of judgement in such matters! When you live on an accretion disk you often need to do reality checks.

NOTE 18 – BEING HEALED – 04/20/2016 – OUTSIDE THE LIBRARY

At about 16:30 pm as I was leaving the Mar Vista Public Library I had one of the more moving and perplexing experiences of my life. As I started to get into my truck a thin young woman, who had been sitting one table away from me and working very diligently on something, ran up to me. She stood very close and said, "Do you mind if I pray for you." (those were her exact words).

I said something that I never expected to hear from me; "Yes, if you wish." She reached down and touched my right leg and then asked God to heal me and make my leg well again. It was astounding to me – she was so genuine, so spiritually motivated – I had not the slightest hesitation or negative reaction. All I could say was "Thank you … really thank you" as she ran off back into the library.

I got in to drive away but I could not escape what had happened. I almost backed into a parked car. Very shortly afterwards I stopped, got out of my truck and began to cry. Not big tears, just a constant flow. As I am writing this I cannot not make them stop.

It is now the next day – I could not continue writing about the incident that had happened just minutes before – I could not sort out what had happened, how and why I had reacted in the unusual manner I did.

All of my normal reactions and anti-religious biases did not come into play. Many years ago, I had been expelled from Roman Catholic Sunday school for pressing the question that I had regarding the Holy Trinity. Specifically, I thought that it wasn't really a trinity but a single person with a multiple personality disorder. My father was furious but it got me out of there permanently since it wasn't the first time I had "caused problems" like suggesting that Mary could not possibly have been a virgin since everybody should know where babies come from. When I was told that the virgin birth was a miracle I said that it was "a miracle she didn't get caught by her parents". That one didn't get me expelled but I remember that comment racked up a ton of Hail Marys.

For all of my adult life I have been an agnostic or uncommitted atheist. My conceit has always been that I was like *Abu Ben Adhem* in the poem by Leigh Hunt:

> Abou Ben Adhem (may his tribe increase!)
>
> Awoke one night from a deep dream of peace,
>
> And saw, within the moonlight in his room,
>
> Making it rich, and like a lily in bloom,

An angel writing in a book of gold:
Exceeding peace had made Ben Adhem bold,
And to the presence in the room he said,
"What writest thou?" The vision raised its head,
And with a look made of all sweet accord,
Answered, "The names of those who love the Lord."
"And is mine one?" said Abou. "Nay, not so,"
Replied the angel. Abou spoke more low,
But cheerly still; and said, "I pray thee, then,
Write me as one that loves his fellow men."

The angel wrote, and vanished. The next night
It came again with a great wakening light,
And showed the names whom love of God had blest,
And lo! Ben Adhem's name led all the rest.

Truth or not, that is always what I have felt or wanted to feel about myself. I have always had a measured faith in the value of mankind or perhaps more of a hope that people would live up to their potential rather than compete at a baser level with other animals.

So, what happened to me? It is really very hard for me to say. I certainly have not changed my basic beliefs but maybe I have finally got to that point in my life to allow the spiritual in myself and to see it in others who are polar opposites of me.

She touched not only my leg but my mind – maybe my soul. I felt this as much as I have felt anything --- one immaculate, private act of faith can be immensely powerful!

NOTE 19 – A MEDICAL MIRACLE

Never ride your bike into a wall at 30 miles per hour! It really, really hurts!

I had just purchased a new recumbent tadpole tricycle (steering wheels at the front) as a personal gift for being somewhat of a fanatic rider on the beach bike paths along Santa Monica Bay. It was fantastic to be able to lay back and put as much power into my legs as possible. No leaning over the handlebars and getting a kink in my neck by trying not to run into anything while I was trying to ride as fast as I could. There were significant differences in cornering and the fact that, because I was recumbent there was not a lot of possibility to shift weight. None-the-less it was great to be able to actually see and appreciate the world as I rode through it.

For the first week, I was just getting used to the feel of it. I was careful and had to get used to several things including the toe clips (actually straps) that I had never used before. However, I rapidly started to pick up the speed on each subsequent day. The straps were needed to keep one's feet on the pedals, which were out and up in front, with the crank set.

Just at the end of our cul-de-sac was a remarkably conveniently placed bicycle path that lead directly to the ocean (about 3.5 km away) and connected to miles of bike path along the coast. The only slight glitch was that one had to ascend a very short steep grade to climb to the path parallel to Ballona Creek. This was only a glitch on the way up but it became a DISASTER on the way down. From the bike path there was a 90 degree turn and another at the bottom to enter the park. There also happened to be a brick wall at the turn.

After my fastest ride by far I rounded the corner quite quickly and did not brake down the grade, perhaps thinking that I could just do that at the bottom … BIG MISTAKE. Braking did not slow me enough and I leaned as hard to the right as I could and pulled my wheels hard over as well. Had I thought about the physics of it I would never have done it since the left wheel immediately dug in, slewed the bike toward the wall and sheared off my left pedal. There would have been absolutely no problem had my foot not been in the pedal when it hit the wall!

The momentum carried the entire bike into the wall but I was able to save the bike and myself by reaching out and pushing off. Now I was at the foot of the wall with a pedal on my foot that was already throbbing with intense pain. When I looked down at my left foot it was very clear to me that I had really "screwed the pooch". The strap had cut right through my shoe. For some insane reason, I tried to stand up to get off the bike. The pain was intense enough to make me see dots and nearly pass out. The only positive thing was that I fell forward, rolled on my shoulder and was on the grass swearing like a drunken sailor. My house was no more than 300 meters from the other side of the park but I had to get there. There was absolutely no way in heaven or hell that I would use my cell phone to call home for help. The first reason was blind pride and the fact that there was no way I was in any humor to discuss what a bonehead I was (am) and the second was that no one was home (a good thing in my addled brain).

I rolled over, got on the bike and used my right leg (my weak one) to pedal home with the help of both hands on the steering wheels that I used more like a wheel-chair. I somehow managed to get the gate opened without getting out of the bike and made my way to the back door that I open from the ground. I pushed the bike toward the garage, slithered through the kitchen right to the bathroom. I then sit myself on the toilet and balanced on my right leg to get into the drugs in the medicine cabinet. There were several older vials of pain killers from previous incidents and my wife's surgery. I immediately took at least two very powerful Vicodin tablets as well as a number of ibuprofen. The swelling was getting out of control very quickly and my foot had completely fill my shoe and swelling was even coming out of the rip that the strap had made in the top of the shoe.

I got back down on the floor, dragged myself into the kitchen, fished for a carving knife and very quickly cut my shoe off. This took very little effort but a great dealing of cursing to counteract the pain. The cupboard was quite a high hurdle at this point but I pulled myself up to the fridge and got all of the ice that I could from the ice maker tray, put it into freezer bags and then put them into a garbage bag that I could drag behind me into the bedroom. I then crawled into bed, got a pillow under my foot, covered myself completely and then tried to think of what would be next. I had several hours before anyone would be home, the pain was settling down and the ice was working to numb everything. The painkillers were also doing the admirable job of shutting down my racing brain. Very shortly afterwards I fell asleep.

When my wife got home she entered the bedroom and immediately thought that I had ridden too far and fell asleep. I said nothing and she asked what I intended to cook since it was my turn. I very calmly told her that it wouldn't be a very good idea if I cooked because it was difficult for me to stand. My response brought the unavoidable series of questions ...

>"Are you OK?"

"Fine."

>"Why can't you stand up?"

"I hurt my foot."

She then picked up the covers from the end of the bed and saw my elevated foot completely wrapped in a towel filled with cold water containing freezer bags. I do not remember what specifically was said but it seemed to be much ado about nothing – or at least nothing I could do anything about myself.

We immediately went to the emergency room of a local small hospital and I was put into a wheel chair, decked out with more ice (as soon as a nurse looked at my foot). Everyone was being very nice and solicitous but that may have been more of a drug side effect than reality. I was indeed the calmest one in the room. As the charge nurse was asking for details a doctor walked by behind her and he clearly heard what the origin of my injury was ... bike accident. The doctor immediately stopped turned and said that he had had his share of bike accidents. This set the stage for a larger spiral in the accretion disk. He asked why I seemed so calm. I told him that I was completely self-medicated and that being upset would not make the breaks go away. He took off one of the icepacks and within about 30 seconds called for an intern to take me to X-ray immediately. This was incredible because we had not even finished the paperwork. My wife took care of that as I was wheeled down the hall. It took no more than 15 minutes and the doctor who had ordered the x-rays came in, turned on the light box and began shaking his head. He was the chief of ER services and turned to me and asked what I thought. I asked him if he meant his head shaking or the x-rays. I told him that they both did not look promising. He then asked me when this had occurred, who my personal physician was and how many other surgeries had I been treated to. He then said he would be back in a few minutes. Since my wife was sent into the room I anticipated at least an hour wait since the ER was full of people. However, in a very few minutes he was back. He had called my doctor and he then said that I had to go home, take more Vicodin, and show up first thing in the morning at the Santa Monica Orthopedic & Sports Medicine Group. He apologized as he said that they were totally incapable of giving me the help I need but he had arranged for me to see one of the best orthopedic specialists in Los Angeles – Dr. Bert Mandelbaum.

I had spent way too much time in hospitals when I was young and can say with considerable authority that this was the fastest response I had ever seen. He said that if I had some time later on he would really like to know how I made such a mess of my foot on a bike.

After some appropriate wifely admonitions and more drugs, I had a reasonable night of sleep and steeled myself for the groping and hopping necessary to get me to my appointment. I had already looked at my laptop regarding bone resorption and reformation times and the time limitations on setting bones ... about 48 to 72 hours.

When we got to the clinic the first surprise of the day was that the orthopedic guru, Dr. Mandelbaum, was on vacation. Great ... I then was introduced to his substitute, an apparently retired surgeon, who didn't bother with a lab coat, and who introduced himself as Dr. John Sellman. The only good thing was that he had a great firm handshake and actually called me by my first name. After looking at my foot for no more than 1 minute he personally wheeled me into a treatment area and told a technician to do an immediate x-ray and what angles he wanted. This was one of the first places to have digital x-rays and the result was very quickly on the computer monitor in the room. Sellman walked in as I was examining my own foot. It was a mess 2 major breaks and more than 50 smaller fractures. The x-ray image attests to this (not very dramatic unless you look more carefully).

Sellman very quickly cut to the chase and asked me to stand up on my right leg. He watched as I fumble to gain balance and lock my knee. He then said, "I thought so ... give me a few of minutes." He left the room; I sat back down in the wheelchair and savored the last bit of Vicodin relief as it was wearing off fast and flinging my foot around for x-rays and examination was not helpful.

There was already something of a minor miracle in the offing because he returned within a few minutes – two doctors in two consecutive days who actually did not leave me waiting for eons. He then asked me a very unusual question, "How would you rate your pain tolerance?".

My response was a bit smart-ass, "It must be high, I have been married twice." He smiled and waited for a more considered response which was "I probably can take any pain until I pass out". There was no boast in this because he had already understood from reading my file that I had many orthopedic surgeries in my youth due to polio and that was also why my right leg was so much weaker than my left. He then said that he had a proposal to make and it was totally my decision as to whether to take it or not. WOW! A doctor who might actually listen to a patient!

He said that although many of his colleagues would opt to operate that he thought that was not only very questionable but might preclude a more creative and natural solution. The damage was severe and my left leg was really my only leg so it had to function very well. He explained the time limitations on bone resorption and how phenomenal the human body was in repairing itself under the right conditions. We discussed resorption for more than a few minutes because of my scientific interests. He then said, "I want to set your foot right now and I have to tell you that this will be incredibly painful but I am confident that this is the best option". I need you to be responsive and communicative while I am doing it so you can't have any painkillers until we are done.

I took all of 30 seconds to say yes – I felt that I had no real option. He then went away and brought back two assistants who were residents in orthopedic surgery. He told them that they may learn something but they would have to hold their questions and be my arm support when he asked me to stand up. They then put a plastic sheet on the floor and Dr. Sellman directed them to put an x-ray source near my foot on the floor and arrange a screen so that he could look at it while he worked.

"So, at first I just want you to put your foot down very lightly but flat … heal and ball touching. The boys will support you and I don't want any wavering or listing. When I tell you, you will have to put your entire weight on it regardless of how much it hurts. Then, I assure you it will hurt even more when I message it into place and wrap it."

It is rare but I was completely speechless. The cast material had already been laid out on the plastic sheet and he was working a ball of plaster in his hands. He then told me to put my foot down on the ball and gently crush it. He moved his hands in to help. It was a surprisingly warm and somewhat comforting feeling as I could feel the heat of the plaster setting. He then told everyone to be ready and me to put my full weight down as he helped press my foot into place. As soon as this happened it was if my tear ducts were directly connected to the nerves in my foot. There was a steady stream down my cheeks and I was even aware that my teeth hurt from clinching them. One of the residents had to pry my fingers off of his arm because I was gripping so hard.

Sellman began to force his fingers into the arch of my foot and shape the rapidly hardening ball. He then started to very aggressively shape my foot against the ball and the floor. I know that at this point I said "Fuck…Fuck …Fuck" and probably a few other choice epithets. He worked incredibly quickly and my cast was finished in a very few minutes. True to his word, one of the residents was injecting morphine into the IV line that they had told me was prophylactic when we started. They guided me back to a gurney and helped me on just as an incredibly rapid wave of relief poured over me. The contrast was incredible and may well explain drug addiction. Sellman had only used latex gloves that he now stripped off. No lab coat, incredibly messy floor, but his suit was pristine. He then told me that it was essential that I "hang around a while". He meant this literally as he told the residents to tie my leg up to the rails holding the ceiling acoustic tiles. As they scrambled around he told one of them to administer the maximum amount of anti-inflammatory possible, apply ice packs and check my toes every five minutes for an hour minimum. He then sat beside me, making sure that the residents were paying attention.

"I have wrapped this foot about as tightly as nature will allow. I shaped the foot to follow the preexisting contour of your arch and finger-aligned the outer compound fracture. We must keep the swelling in check until everything calms down. With a little bit of luck and some patience from you I am pretty sure that you really will mend well."

After several hours of being strapped to the ceiling and watching bad TV (courtesy of the residents who were very directly instructed to get me what I needed) my only complaint is that when I asked for a Cuba Libre they ignored me.

Before setting up on the floor for the sculpting he had asked me what color cast I would like and I very quickly answered "warning orange" like the traffic cones. I got home in a wheel chair because I had to keep it elevated for several days. My daughter loved the color and wanted to be the first to sign a message on the cast.

The message was totally justified but the manner of delivery is a cognitive signature of my daughter who wrote on my new orange cast "Orange: / Warning – / Stupidity / ♥ Rila". As proof, I offer my elegantly polished orange toenails (on swollen toes decorated by same daughter) and my newly signed cast in the accompanying photo. I preferred not to have any other messages on it as the one already there was clear enough for everyone.

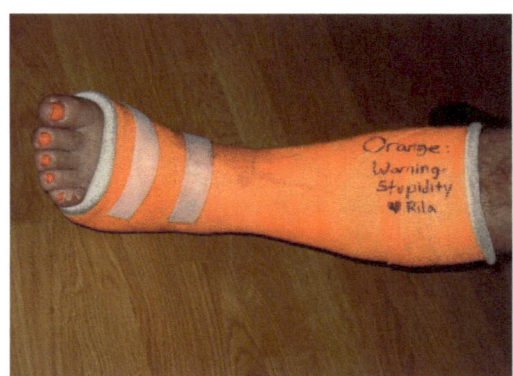

In two weeks, I went back for a follow-up and Sellman was not there. Mandelbaum was back from vacation and as he sat down to look at the x-rays that I had already been studying he got on the phone and told his secretary that we seemed to have cued up the wrong file. I interrupted him and said no that is my foot, I swear that I would know it almost anywhere except for the fact the major breaks were only immediately visible if you knew where to look. It was astounding! The healing was occurring at a ridiculous pace and Mandelbaum was doing another uncharacteristic head shake. He said (and I believe that this is very accurate), "You were very lucky that I was away because I probably would have operated and that would have been a big mistake for both of us. Sellman is amazing!"

That summarized it all. Dr. John Sellman was amazing, ballsie and capable of pulling off something of a miracle.

Within the week, I had crafted an adaptor for my foot so that I could use my new quick releases on my repaired bike and get back out into the world – a little wiser I hoped. Within four more weeks I was walking on it just fine and I do believe that he actually gave me a better and stronger foot than I had.

This note totally reflects my position around the Existential Black Hole. I could have fallen in but instead, I am rewarded for a totally bonehead act. I "accidentally" get at least two doctors who were top notch and unafraid to do what others wouldn't. My healing was much faster than if I had endured an operation and I got a great tale to tell as well.

NOTE 20 – HOME SCHOOLING

I first became aware of home schooling after my daughter Rila made a surprising request to be home schooled. She was in about the middle of grade three in an expensive private school in Culver City. We had legitimately tried the LA public school system and the attempts varied from more focus on personal body armor and drug prevention programs in grade one or full Spanish immersion (i.e. virtually no English speakers except my daughter).

Her complaint was that she was not being "challenged". She knew full well that this was going to depress one of my hot buttons. We discussed the topic for a while but I dismissed it given the fact that it was presented more in a whining manner than as a proposal. However, it did spark me to do some of my own research and it was very enlightening. In most of the United States home schooling seemed (at least at a first glance) to be strongly associated with the Christian Right and their delusional notion that evolution doesn't exist and that the world is about 8000 years old.

Upon further probing, there were legitimate co-operatives of parents who were serious about education and interaction with their children. Many of these groups were markedly more associated with larger urban areas that had distinct problems in providing a decent level of primary education. At this point I was satisfied that spending in excess of $15,000 per child per year for the private school was more than adequate.

After a few months, the requests continued and intensified to the point that I finally had to invoke the "no whining rule". This was a self-protective rule that I had instituted from when my daughter had first asked for Barbie dolls. It consisted of crossing ones opposing fingers (or arms, depending on how large the NO was to be) to indicate an X meaning that whining would get you nothing. The implicit and explicit rules of the game/interaction were that the argument for whatever you want would have to be accompanied by an "account". The account could be a total fabrication but the essential characteristic of any account is that it had to be entertaining and internally consistent (like a good science fiction story).

My daughter really took affront at the fact that I would cut off her legitimate request for home schooling. I very clearly remember what I said to her; "Prove to me that home schooling is a good idea". Thankfully this curtailed the discussion for at least one week. She came back to me and asked how she could prove it to me. Again, I gave her what most people would consider a cryptic answer but she very much understood what I meant; "Prove it to me in a way in which I would understand." This was the first phase of one of the larger ventures of my life that I "did not think through" clearly.

About one week later she came to me and she wanted to learn to use spreadsheets. I really did not associate her request with anything other than a lust for learning powerful new things ... right up my alley (foolish, foolish, father). We began with the basics but I insisted that she learn how to use the mathematical and statistical functions that could make most of her school work a cake-walk. Much to her credit, she knuckled down and began to show some aptitude for manipulating data.

Rila's campaign toward home schooling began in earnest when she ran into a research problem at her school library. She was supposed to do a country report on any country of her choice. She had already travelled to several counties in Europe and that was of no interest to her so she decided that Mongolia would be good. I gave her an enthusiastic thumb up ... Genghis Khan ... the Golden Horde ... world domination... great stuff! The next day she came back from school and reported that the head librarian (a retiree but graduate of UCLA) told her that Mongolia was no longer a country. I was completely taken aback. I generally pride myself on having a vast array of factual knowledge of questionable utility and I could not understand how I had missed the demotion of Mongolia.

The lead page of my "Memo" is reproduced below (there were 25 pages of attachments) – the only change made was the redacted name of the librarian. Ms. Clarke was Rila's beloved home-room teacher so her name was left in but I redacted the name of the librarian.

"**DATE:** April 22, 2002

TO: Katherine Clarke & [LIBRARIAN]

FROM: Dr. Duane R. Chartier

RE: **Existence of Mongolia**

Rila has seemingly caused some debate as to the existence of Mongolia as a country.

If Mongolia is indeed not a country then I strongly suggest that the management at EHS immediately contact:

I. the government of the said republic - send correspondence to the appropriate addressees at the Mongolian Embassy to the United States, 2833 M Street, Washington, D.C.; (202) 333-7117 or in the capital, Ulaanbaatar (transliterated and variously spelled including Ulanbator, Ulan Bator, Ulaan Bator, etc.).
II. the US State Department (see attached nine pages of notes on Mongolia)
III. the CIA (see attached nine pages). I do not suggest contacting the CIA directly because they are in the habit of misplacing countries or is that destabilizing them??
IV. the United Nations (see attached 7 pages) who will be saddened to hear that the membership of Mongolia in the UN since October 27, 1961 has been a sham.

In general, you can be assured that Rila knows approximately 85% of world capitals and is not prone to make up new ones since her father gets a little steamed.

There are 438 listed books on Mongolia on amazon.com and we will donate at least one to the library after the country reports are completed.

_____
Duane R. Chartier"

A year later (in her fifth grade) she came to me and asked me if you could divide by zero. I was very intrigued and I almost immediately jumped on the question and said, "Absolutely but the answers will be very interesting!" The bait had been dropped in the water and I had swallowed it, the hook and, the entire rod and reel. She then quasi-innocently offered that her math teacher had told her that you couldn't divide by zero. I was incensed, not at the tuition, but by the fact that someone who actually had a degree in mathematics would say something so patently stupid and wrong.

I got on my computer and produced a one page memo to the particular teacher with 26 pages of attachments. The exact memo (to her home room teacher – not the math teacher … name withheld) follows:

"DATE: February 5, 2003

TO: Kim Wynn

FROM: Duane R. Chartier

RE: Division by Zero

While proofing Rila's math homework the other night I was surprised at my own reaction to the statement on the page header that "division by zero is impossible". I proceeded to discuss this with Rila who held the notion that if it was in the book it was correct and that I was just being my old critical self. The fact is that the notion of division by zero is not so simple as a trivial definition might indicate and is still the topic of serious consideration in mathematics.

Please look at the attachments and I hope that you will see that this is indeed a very interesting topic and can be very fruitful to explore so that the children will understand that mathematics is not simply arithmetic and that assumptions must always be examined. The fascinating properties of 0, 1 and ∞ are often overlooked even by mathematicians.

My experience as a scientist is that it is wholly unwise to teach anyone concepts that will have to be discarded later because we were too busy to address the bigger picture. What I have also generally found with children is that since their concepts are not yet set in stone it is often possible to get them to accept some very counterintuitive and difficult things.

Given the equation $n/0 = x$ (where $n \neq 0$) …

    1. The standard (and wholly inadequate response) is that it is impossible to divide by zero. This is the case if one takes the most limited, unimaginative and unproductive view of real numbers and set theory. However, there is a very different answer …

2. As one proceeds to predict the quotient of the limits of 2 functions where the limit of the denominator is 0 at ∞ then the answer is ∞. The problem arises because infinity is not a number but rather a set, operator or other entity. This is certainly the most useful solution and the admonition to students should perhaps be that division by zero leads to an entirely new mathematics ... ***Transfinite Mathematics*** as introduced by Gregor Cantor in the late 19th century.

I won't even start to address the marvelous difficulties of 0/0 = 1 or indeterminate or ∞???

However, just the mere discussion of the paradox is a potential educational opportunity."

One of the attachments was a recent Ph.D. thesis by a Finn on the consequences of division by 0.

This communication received no response at all from either the home room teacher or the math teacher (cc'ed) or the principal of the school. Perhaps that is no surprise – SOME PEOPLE DON'T LIKE NOTHING, 0, whatever!

As she progressed through grade five I realized I was in trouble when she wanted to show me how extensive her spreadsheet skills had become. She had found the proper method and tools to convince me. She calculated tuition, time lost to our business, school down time and efficiency ... Needless-to-say, I was eventually cornered. I said that I was convinced and would draft my own proposal for her to sign. However, I made it clear that she had another challenge – to convince her mother, Susi (also my business partner).

Her method was admirably devious. She asked if she could plan a lunch with an older girl who had a black belt in Tae-Kwan-Do and who was a real role model for Rila and the girl's mother has well my wife, Susi. The girl was 14 years old and had never been to an actual school and was incredibly poised. The point of this was to have Susi as a captive audience with witnesses as to the efficacy and intelligence of home schooling. I couldn't have chosen a better strategy myself. Rila booked lunch at a relatively outré restaurant at Santa Monica Airport called Typhoon. Of course, she intended to illustrate how sophisticated she was by ordering a dish from their insect menu (seriously! – we had SINGAPORE STYLE SCORPIONS (shrimp toast) and TAIWANESE CRICKETS (stir fried, raw garlic, chili pepper, Asian basil)).

The lunch went ahead as did the inevitable outcome of Rila's plan to bulldoze her parents. Within a week, she had the go-ahead from mom. My only response was to have her sign a contract with me indicating that she clearly understood the consequences of her action and that my role was not as a teacher but as a consultant. She would choose the path and rate of learning with some input from both parents.

My wife did not approve of the entire contract notion but I contended that it had a larger value in pointing out that one owns what one does and that many things in life have both personal and legal consequences and significance. It is also consistent with a belief I have always had that empowerment is good - one cannot expect responsibility without authority. The day of the contract signing was the first day of the most significant education that I have ever received.

Rila completed high school equivalency in California at age 15 and my son Raef completed his at 14.5 years old. This was not a result of studying for the test, innate brilliance, or even particularly hard work. It was about the ownership they had in their own future and their real input into what future it would or could be.

Learning is possible, it often happens despite our effort, I am just unsure that teaching is possible. I am personally convinced that we must customize the learning experience not package it and pretend that learning has occurred. Learning and teaching must be bilateral - the model of teacher and student is ancient and no longer adequate for us to move forward. These things I know from many years of teaching and/or mentoring. The entire home schooling experience with my daughter and son taught me as much about human relations as about education. I belatedly thank both of my children for their patience and guidance and I apologize for my plentiful deficiencies.

NOTE 21 – THE SOLAR CYCLE AND THE PROBLEMS WITH INCOMPLETE RESEARCH

Before I write about an indelible mark I made upon my daughter's consciousness I need to counterbalance it with one of the few definitively positive contributions that I made to my children's education ... "Crater Day". It was certainly my favorite day at school ever[11]! I spend about 20 hours making about four hours of lectures and setting up real experiments in the back yard. The intent was to show the difference between impact craters and volcanic craters and show examples not only from earth but on other heavenly bodies. Even our lunch was used for experimentation. On the patio table a large stainless steel bowl was laden with a flattened mass of mashed potatoes. Then all of the people attending were encouraged to throw meatballs (3 each) at whatever velocity and angle they desired and then measure the crater or take a picture before devouring the evidence. I have my doubts whether the technical points made any impression but the flying meatballs most certainly did!

Now I am free to write about the seamier side of being an "educational consultant". Both children had long and short term projects that they were interested in and had a fundamental part of designing. The long-term projects always required some research component (both Internet and library) as well as a PowerPoint presentation to an invited audience. Rila wanted to do a project on the Aurora Borealis. My initial response was that it would be insufficiently instructive and challenging as a project and that she would have to have a harder core component. After a few days, she came back to me and indicated that she would include the Aurora Australis (southern lights). I expressed my displeasure by simply looking over my glasses and waving her off. Needless-to-say I got her return patented eye-roll and an admonishing:

"Daddy!" So, what is your problem? I doubled the project".

"NO. You doubled the title and did nothing to make it any more challenging or informative other than you decided to count the South pole as somewhat significant".

She went off miffed but came back in a couple of hours and wanted to discuss what she could do. In her mind that meant that I was going to tell her. I had finally learned enough about the home schooling experience that I decided to take my punishment like a man and not to just lay out HER project. The initial discussion was more like a contest in who could pause the longest without saying anything of value. I then suggested that even someone who had done the "most limited research" would be able to

---

[11] As I started writing this note (04/30/2016) I texted my son and daughter to see what was their most memorable experience in home schooling and within a few minutes Rila answered Crater Day. I will admit that I probably really tainted the survey by asking, with my typically warped sense of puns, "Can you remember anything from home schooling that made an impression on you?"

tell me something about the importance of solar wind. She went away for a few hours and came back telling me that solar wind was guided into the poles and created the spectacular displays of light and color. My response was very terse "guided solar wind … interesting". That abruptly ended discussion section one. She was yet again miffed.

Several days later we entered into a more productive discussion of the development of the topic. She had spent some time bothering to find out what solar wind was – about 1 million miles per hour ionized particles (usually protons … hydrogen nuclei). She then provided the essential information that the earth's magnetic field was the guiding force that brought it into the poles. At this point I was more prepared to be helpful. I told her that I would be asking myself a series of questions and that she might like to listen:

> What happens when the solar wind contact with the atmosphere?
>
> What causes the variation in color?
>
> Do we always see the aurorae?
>
> Is the magnetic field uniform?
>
> How does magnetism effect everything?

She went away quite pleased that she felt that she had caused me to map out her approach.

A few more days passed and she came back with an outline of the presentation and wanted my opinion. My only comment on the single page of point-form regurgitation from sources was, "I think you should change the title and the emphasis". This provoked a kind of harrumph and she was yet again off in a bit of a snit.

Shortly afterward she returned and yet again tried to get me to craft her new title and approach. She said that she could go into more depth on solar wind. My only comment was that it didn't seem to be too "deep" a topic. That only left the magnetic field of earth as the other fundamental element. She immediately leapt on this as if it was a pot of gold left by a leprechaun. I agreed that she could indeed talk much more about the earth's magnetic field. She then left with a much more positive demeanor.

A few days more work produced a written interim report that she wanted me to look at. I took it and was generally impressed by the ease of writing and that fact that she had been careful not to mouth every source without giving it her own character and voice. I finally got to something that I am much more attuned to – a graph. In this case, it was a very clean and exceptionally tight linear graph (in fact, there were no error bars) of the change in the earth's magnetic field that traced the earth's age back 8000 years to zero! Anyone who has done actual science understands fundamentally that real data is messy and when something stands out so clearly it is either a miracle (Nobel Prize) or a huge fiction.

I immediately suspected where she had lifted the data from but I really wanted to hear her take so I started to probe a bit. "Why is the graph only limited to 8000 years? Don't you think it is a little odd that the earth had no magnetic field 8000 years ago?" She did not take too kindly to me forcing her to examine the quoted source in much more detail on my computer. As I suspected it was taken from a religious site that has as much to do with science as Bugs Bunny has to do with actual rabbits. This began a multi-hour (over several days) intensive discussion of what was acceptable as a data source and, more particularly how to look at data in a somewhat objective manner. I don't exactly remember what I had to say about the specific website or the people who were insane enough to post such unmitigated bullshit but I believe it was most likely quite forceful and not lacking in seedy epithets.

This was actually a very critical moment in the entire educational landscape – sources and reliability. It is particularly a problem in the new world of the Internet where even my cat could have a website where it might launch outrageous misinformation campaigns about rodents like mice or the Easter Bunny. Just because a website looks pretty does not mean anything whatever in the realm of veracity. After many, many, many examples of looking at websites and the data presented together with my children I think that I had finally made some fundamental point – it is often important not only what you are looking at but who produced it and why. Without ever talking about the earth's magnetic field I sent her back to do a better job of researching her planned presentation.

The next iteration of interaction between us was very much more what I was hoping for. She had taken my comments (criticisms) to heart and became very much more conscious of sources. Her next stab at the magnetic field was the correct one in that the data originated from the USGS website.[12] It was very clear that the earth's magnetic field was changing constantly and that it had flipped several times over history. She had also targeted data that showed that the field strength was lessening at the fastest recorded rate in history ... very cool. So now we were getting to a revised title. With a little verbal help, she changed it to "The Aurora Borealis and the Earth's Waning Magnetic Field". This seemed to be a very much more appropriate level.

With a newfound interest in the phenomenon Rila adopted her evolved strategy of getting what she wanted so she suggested that we travel to Canada to observe the aurora rather than looking at pictures. The only relatives that I have live in Winnipeg, Manitoba – one of the coldest inhabited places on the planet (just one of many personally held opinions and reasons I do not live there)! After a little coaxing of her mother we were off to "The Great White North" for Christmas of 2004.

---

[12] United States Geological Survey – www.usgs.gov

It was bitterly cold when we landed and I, who had once lived in Canada, was no more prepared for it than my hapless family. We had packed our warmest clothes in our suitcases rather than having them ready to wear. There is a saying, the origin of which I do not know, but when we landed in Winnipeg at -49°C I blurted it out "It's cold enough to freeze the balls off a brass monkey!" It even hurt to say it at that temperature. It warmed up over several days to the relatively balmy temperature of -31°C. My son, Raef, who was training for his black belt in Tae-Kwan-Do decided that he wanted to provide the Master with proof of his determination and this led to him racing out bare-footed and bare-chested for the very briefest pose for the accompanying photograph.

He ended up taking 30 minutes to warm up again – silly skinny bugger!

So here we all are freezing our asses off and trying to get to know relatives who some had never met before. There was only one night without complete cloud cover and there was not the merest hint of an aurora!

Upon our return from the frigid trip Rila and I discussed (my idea) the rather critical issue of solar min and solar max – something completely missing from her interim report. After a couple of days Rila had no problem articulating why she thought that I had failed as a consultant ... I think that she really meant father. My only statement was, "Limited research will always get you into trouble." Concise and not comforting but fundamentally true. In my opinion she had failed in her job to be a real student.

So, both Rila and I are left with some issues:

- Mine is how could anyone do even the smallest bit of legitimate research on the aurora and not realize that they were at "solar min", the minimum in solar activity for flares and sunspot that basically only occurs every 11 (to 14 years)? At the end of 2004 solar activity was ramping down very strongly. In fact, the coming couple of years became some of the quietest on record with very few solar flares for nearly a year – therefore very few aurorae.
- Rila's is how could her father (not educational consultant) allow her to travel to the Great White North (Winnipeg), potentially freeze off body parts, have to deal with one uncle who wanted to convert her, and not see the aurora?

My only defense is that I have nothing to do with gross solar activity and I did not distract her in any way from doing her research. There is always a cost when one cuts corners or fails to be properly informed. The cost here is that she may never visit Canada again …. Burrrrrr. Somehow, I have a strong feeling that she does not see this as a negative. The real loss is missing the aurora on this planet or on others in the solar system[13] – it is a fabulous thing! I even remember hearing the crackling in the atmosphere in some god-forsaken place in northern Manitoba when I was very young. It was awe-inspiring.

---

[13] Jupiter has spectacular aurorae due to its very strong magnetic field. These are only visible in the ultraviolet but that is why we have technology. See https://www.spacetelescope.org/images/opo9632a/ retrieved 07/16/2016.

NOTE 22 – HOME SCHOOLING – POINTS NEVER MADE … POINTS TAKEN

In the other notes on home schooling I have presented things, more-or-less accurately, that really happened. This is much more a metaphorical note on things that perhaps should have happened or that I completely missed to elevate or failed to properly introduce.

I had texted both my children to ask them their most memorable moments in home schooling and it was very clearly the day we spent on impact versus volcanic craters. While gratifying (since I loved it too) I found myself trying to reconstruct an unreconstructable time series of events and influences.

Of all of the things that I discussed with my children one of the most significant to me was a small paper, or perhaps better characterized as an opinion piece, by Marvin Minsky a true legend in the field of artificial intelligence. The paper titled *Matter, Mind and Models*[14] is only a few pages but is profound in its depth and cuttingly incisive in its understanding of the human condition.

"When intelligent machines are constructed, we should not be surprised to find them as confused and as stubborn as are men in their convictions about mind-matter, consciousness, free will, and the like. For all such questions are pointed at explaining the complicated interactions between parts of the self-model. A man's or a machine's strength of conviction about such things tells us nothing about the man or about the machine except what it tells us about his model of himself."

We spent a couple of days on this and I should have got the message from my wife that I was probably navigating in the deep end of the pool and with no references to my audience. I had hoped that Marvin would have influenced them in a similar manner to his influence on me but that was clearly not the case.

The lasting effects of Marvin Minsky on my messy mind! Curse you Marvin … bastard computer scientist … rogue philosopher … second-guesser of second-guessers! I hold Marvin personally responsible for my problems with living on the accretion disk in a universe with ever-changing models of self and diabolically shifting points of reference. I have always believed that a deep and fundamental knowledge of almost anything is ultimately much more useful than a "Trivial Pursuit" approach to learning and the world. I also have always known that this is not a formula for success but there it is. **So … ironically, in failing to show the profundity and importance of Marvin Minsky's thoughts to my children I inadvertently contributed to their ultimate success in the world.**

Sometimes living on the accretion disk is very useful when values get inverted.

---

[14] https://groups.csail.mit.edu/medg/people/doyle/gallery/minsky/mmm.html

Having just waxed poetic on perceived failure perhaps I should try to be a little more balanced and positive on some good things that do happen. Regardless of what other educators, mentors, teachers ... whatever, think - I personally believe that poetry is one of the higher achievements in any language so it was one of the very few things that I insisted upon. Our work on poetry was no more than 4 or 5 days but it certainly made a lasting impression on me. The only input that I had was to stipulate a very general topic (directive) and sometimes the metrical form.

The following poem is submitted with the permission of the author, Raef Chartier, who completed in at the ripe old age of 16.46 years. This work was all of his choosing since we had completed home schooling in the formal sense and it was well after the initial introduction to poetry.

The Bearded Lady   Directive: Sense   Raef Chartier - © 9/28/2012

I drive along and see the carnival
In its sights I revel
My eye falls upon a maiden
Her hair thick and laden

I approach her to talk
As she turns I gawk
At a carnival it's not weird
For I see she has a beard

To touch and feel
Perceive something as real
I ask if I may touch
She does not mind much

I squeeze her beard in hand
I feel how soft and grand
I ask her out to a date
And she says she can not wait

I take the bearded lady
to a cafe that is shady
we order our food
we pour the wine set the mood

Our food comes in
and we say chin chin
in her beard lodges food
but it tastes kind of good

Although it may seem strange
the love we share can not change
I never ask her to shave
and she enjoys it when I misbehave

We cherish our true love
something you can't be rid of
making no sense and quite novel
I love the bearded lady of the carnival.

Perhaps this is a much better connection or point to be made than one about the existential problems associated with Marvin Minsky, *Matter, Mind and Models* ... and artificial intelligence.

NOTE 23 - FAMILY – CAN'T LIVE WITH THEM ... CAN'T KILL 'EM

Due to a bit of a freak of nature I was effectively an only child or perhaps more like an abandoned child or an orphan. Please NO SYMPATHY ... LET ME EXPLAIN ... It's all inverted, like the rest of my life. I contracted polio when I was 9 months old, just as the vaccines became available in 1952-53, so I spent the better part of my youth in hospital for various surgeries. What is truly inverted is that most of my family consider it my good luck to have contracted polio! YES, and bizarrely, ironically, I have come to agree! They lived in a hostile environment and many of them seem to have very deep emotional scars and what anyone might call PTSD[15] and/or Stockholm Syndrome[16].

One of my brothers, without any consultation with me whatsoever, and without the tiniest substantive piece of evidence surmised that I was having an affair with his wife of twenty years. I only found out after trying to get him to answer several phone messages that I had left while I was visiting from over 1528.47 miles (2459.77 kilometers away – give or take 10 or 15 depending on where you are). WOW!

Initially I was incredibly hurt and pissed off but as that passed (since he would not talk to me or communicate in any other way) I began to ponder how such a supposition could manifest itself. What is truly incredible is that of all of the persons I have known I am one of the least well equipped and skilled to venture into the territory of other people's emotions and motivations. The plain truth of it is that I so seldom even understand my own emotions that it would be very foolish, unproductive and possibly damaging to speculate on how others come to personal decisions. However, I felt that such a wild accusation deserved an equally inane and unbalanced approach! The ironic twist is that I had nothing to say. There were just so many questions pulsing through my brain:

- How could anyone who really didn't know me accuse me of such sleazy and underhanded behavior?
- How could a "family" member think this?
- Have I an international reputation for immorality that I had somehow missed?
- Do I have an impeccable record for seducing married women (also one I was not aware of)?
- Have I ever done anything heinous to my brother? AH THAT MUST BE IT ...!

I MUST HAVE DONE SOMETHING TERRIBLE TO HIM (again, something that I am completely unaware of) to have merited such an *ad-hominem* attack on my character.

I do remember being about 10 years old (he was 7 or 8) and I made him kneel with his hands behind his head – execution style. This was done at pistol-point - only a CO_2 pellet gun. The argument was over who had destroyed a model battleship that took me over 100 hours to make. When his final answer was that it was my fault for leaving it out in the first place I summarily "executed him". I shot him in the ass

---

[15] Post-Traumatic Stress Disorder
[16] Stockholm Syndrome. I am positive that one of my sisters has late onset Stockholm Syndrome. If this is not an officially recognized mental health condition, it should be! There is an interesting hypothesis ... proposal that has an extended interpretation of Stockholm Syndrome to persons in abusive relationships.

(because I felt he was a gigantic one!) and it did draw a bit of blood. Frankly, not nearly enough. That lead to my immediate incarceration by my mother, who took away my wheelchair for 1 week, and the permanent loss of my prized and previously secret weapon. That is the only significant interaction I can remember from childhood involving my brother but after 53 long years he was now able to exact his revenge by besmirching my generally good name. Holy crap 53 years – one would get less of a sentence for first degree murder! He must have been incredibly mad for so very long. I really had not remembered the incident until now.

WAIT! WAIT A DAMN MINUTE! This isn't about ME although I generally prefer things to be about me. Although disappointing, it is quite enlightening to look at the situation from a different perspective. I would love to be able to say that it was from "his perspective" but that would be very disturbing as I would have to adopt a completely alien, inane, and self-destructive persona.

My brother has something really, fundamentally, wrong with his model of himself in the world. He seems to see himself as a victim and everyone is picking on him and perhaps even plotting against him and standing in his path for success and happiness. There are probably operationally sound hypotheses as to how this occurred. One of the major elements that comes to mind is having an abusive family environment. I remember joking with other family members about his obsession with our mother being a Nazi. I do very vaguely remember her assertions of her Austrian origin but that should be no surprise. I don't think you could find more than three living Austrians who will admit that they greeted Hitler with open arms. So how did Hitler take over Austria without one drop of blood? Enough with delusions and history … onto delusions and the present!

My brother … I wish I could throttle him and I wish I could help him … the cruel reality is that I can do neither. In fact, I am the least likely person capable of affecting any change at all. I seem to be his neurotic push button. I can only speak for myself --- all change comes from within and usually at a considerable cost. The existential answer that I managed to get out of the craziness is that most people likely have someone in their life like this.

NOTE 24 – DYSFUNCTIONALITY IS THE NEW "NORMAL"

For many years I was led to believe that my family was reasonably rare in being almost totally dysfunctional. This is such a load of bullocks!

Just for the hell of it I asked a single simple question of a cross-section of people who I have come to know through the inordinate time I spend at the gym. They spanned the ages from 22 through 82 and there were 10 in total. The question was posed exactly as below:

"YES or NO answer only. Do you know anyone with what you would call a "normal" family?"

100% replied NO. This was indeed a small group (10) but think of the odds of throwing heads on a coin 10 time in a row … ($\frac{1}{2} \times \frac{1}{2} \times \frac{1}{2} \times \frac{1}{2} \times \frac{1}{2} \times \frac{1}{2} \times \frac{1}{2} \times \frac{1}{2} \times \frac{1}{2} \times \frac{1}{2}$ = 1/1024). 1 in 1024 is the chance of this randomly happening! The answers I received were as far from random as statistics allows - NOT RANDOM ALL – a real perception that "Normal" is indeed NOT NORMAL it is DYSFUNCTIONAL.

So now I am completely perplexed. I never wanted to discuss my family due to my complete lack of understanding of how it functions or is supposed to function and now, late in life, I find out that there is no masterplan or model and most people just muddle through and generally make up shit about their family interactions. CRAP!

One of my exes contends that she is from a loving and close family but whenever they get together I would stake any amount of money on potentially dangerous friction within about 2 days. Whenever I dared to say anything my family was immediately used as the poster children for dysfunctionality – a point I never debated at the time but, in the wisdom of hindsight, my own family is a lot easier to read, predict and avoid, as is often necessary.

This kind of protective reaction of family relations is quite understandable. One of the more powerful unifying forces in many battling families is to have an outsider attack or criticize one of them. There is a "closing of ranks" or what I like to call the "get the wagons in a circle reaction" like in the old Westerns when the savages are threatening the wagon train. This has always been a little hypocritical and perverse to me since it translates to "We can beat up on them (our own family) but you can't!" All that one has to do is consider the number of sayings related to family interactions… bad blood, black sheep, skeletons in the closet… I need not belabor this but the list is potentially massive.

It now seems very clear to me that **families are really meta-models for bullies.** This would explain a great deal!

NOTE 25 – "LILIAM INTER SPINAS" – ROMANCE ON THE ROCKS

At best of times communication between people can be difficult but if one adds distance, anticipation and hormones it can quickly go spiraling out of control.

I had decided that after 25 years of marriage (the second one that ended in February of 2014) that my learning curve was quite flat and that I would definitely not fall in love again. I should not have to reiterate flat learning curve but it seems particularly appropriate for this note. Given the fact that I had chosen to visit Winnipeg (a long way from LA) to try to connect with family that I had not grown up with should have alerted me to my fundamental learning disability.

Before 2014, I had only been to Canada once every 11 years (the solar cycle and limited research ... another note). I had an art installation in St. Paul and decided that there was no legitimate excuse for not stopping by when I was already so close. It was January and VERY cold, but I was warmly welcomed and that compensated for the climatic conditions. Prior to this visit, almost all of the information I had received regarding my family had been positive. Suddenly, I became one of the family and the floodgates opened! I was party to all of the infighting, gossip, and character assassination typical of English tabloids. To say TMI was a vast understatement.

I have six siblings, who are clearly the result of a handsome and over-sexed French Catholic father and an "Austrian" mother who had failed to realize the basic necessity of birth control (albeit surreptitious if you are Catholic). There are two elder sisters and then three brothers and another sister.

I have never believed that trashing people behind their back was anything but cowardly. My personal philosophy is that I will never stab anyone in the back. If I am going to stab anyone it will be in the chest and they will definitively know I am coming. They will generally be the only people who will know why since my disputes are with them ... not the general public. All of this is an addendum to yet another note on family (my brother). This note is about love, real love ... the amazing rollercoaster!

As I was sitting in the living room of my sister Celeste, I was completely blindsided by a comment she made; "Are you going to call Lynn ... she thinks highly of you?". I was having a glass of wine, turned quizzically towards her and said, "Who the hell is Lynn and - nobody thinks highly of me?!" She then offered the essential qualifying data. "You know Lynn ... from 40 years ago."

My attitude and posture immediately changed. I sat straight up as if I had been slapped in the back of the head. I had an immediate mental picture of Lynn ... crystalline and all too clear. Even more disturbing to me was that I have rarely remembered any of the details of many of the women I have dated, seen ... slept with, but she was amazingly present in my consciousness. It had been about forty years prior and I was in Winnipeg for a couple of days to visit just before going to graduate school in chemistry at McMaster University.

I appeared at my sister's house and she was already hosting a young woman for the weekend for the "social". I had no idea what a social was and she told me that people would raise money for something they needed or wanted by having a party and selling tickets. It was completely out of my experience but (to be polite) I decided to go. One incentive was that she introduced me to Lynn... piercingly blue eyes, blond, gorgeous, and affable. We hit it off immediately and then the strangest set of events unfolded. Both of us were together sleeping on a hide-away bed in my sister's home. I think that Lynn was a little inebriated but she seemed to handle me pretty well. Perhaps it was a bad choice putting her in a bed in the living room with me! We made love ... lust ... I woke up early and got on a plane. I don't remember saying goodbye but I had the very strong feeling of running away!

I was absolutely not prepared to be in love ever again! My first great love had died four years before in a motorcycle accident and there was no way I wanted to feel that pain and loss ever again. So, unpleasant alternative, be a complete dick-head, turn your back, never communicate – unfortunately all too easy! I had a new life with the potential purity of the shield of academia – loads of work, no time for a normal life or love, just cheap and rapid sex.

So, there I was on my sister's couch, glass of wine in hand, gazing at my own mental movie. It really did not include a scene where I came off looking like anything but a jerk. Upon the second prompting by my sister to call Lynn I said absolutely nothing. Within a few minutes, she emerged from the kitchen with a piece of paper that she handed to me. It had "Lynn" with a phone numbers and an e-mail. Wordlessly I took it and put it in my pocket as I took another mouthful of wine. It was September (2015) and I was to leave in a couple of days. The paper seemed to be burning a hole in my pocket so I finally relented and one day before I was supposed to leave I called and left a very brief message; "Hello Lynn, it's Duane, I don't know if you remember me this is my number..."

Next day – no call. I called again and left a more testy and challenging message; "Lynn, this is Duane from forty years ago. I manned up ... so should you!" Perhaps it should have been no surprise that this message was not returned. I got on the plane fully exonerated from forty years of avoidance and confident in my righteousness. Despite that initial relief, I returned to LA and I was pissed off – How dare she not respond; especially if she did think so highly of me! So, I sent a snarky and obnoxious e-mail. Still no response.

I was in the gym early the next morning and Victor (a very nice lawyer who works out almost every day) asked me how my trip was. My response was exactly this: "Victor, is it possible for me to sue my Canadian relatives for PTSD treatments?" He told me that it was not his specialty and he didn't think it would be possible although it was a great idea. I was glad to be out of the battle zone of my family and the mine field of guilt associated with a one night stand from forty years before.

A couple of days later my sister called me and told me that I should call Lynn. I told her that I had tried and was "brutally rebuffed" (a marvelous quote from *Clueless*). She said that there was some misunderstanding and that I should call. I left it for one day and then called. Lynn very properly answered the phone and told me that she did not answer calls with unknown area codes. Well and good but "What about my e-mail?" She said, very matter-of-factly, that the e-mail was pretentious and annoying and that she was not going to answer it.

At this point the years between us began to rapidly disappear and our daily, multi-hour conversations became much more intimate and sometimes openly sexual. She sent me a picture of her at her recent 60th birthday. WOW ... all I could say when I spoke to her is that she was "HOT!" I might have even said "smoking hot" but I am not sure – I was clearly not of sound mind! I asked her if I could visit and when. She took a couple of days to finally answer and then told me that I could come when it was convenient. Within one hour I had booked tickets to return to Winnipeg (from October 26 to November 2, 2015) within about one month of having been there for the first time since 2004 (11 years – my "normal" solar cycle for visiting family). We mutually decide to keep my visit a secret from my family for two reasons:

MINE: I had no desire to navigate my family's self-declared war zones. I still had residual PTSD! We needed to have the time together to see if we really could be together.

HERS: She had no idea how long she could tolerate me. In one of our long telephone conversations she told me that I "vomit" everything up verbally. I was initially offended but I had to realize that she was absolutely correct. Talking with her had opened up the floodgates that had been closed for many years. She was probably suffering measurably from TMI Syndrome (Too Much Information).

The next event in our new relationship – flowers - became a very large problem! I decided that because I was irrationally attracted to her that I would send her flowers. I called a florist in Winnipeg and had a long discussion about what I wanted. I wanted 3 white lilies amongst distinctly shorter red roses with several thorny rose stems of the same size. The only message associated with them read "'*Lilium Inter Spinas*'. An iconographic allusion to you, in my mind, in the world."[17]

She received the flowers but on 10/03/2015, I got an e-mail that pierced my heart ...

    "They are really quite beautiful. Thank you, Duane.

---

[17] "*lilium inter spinas*" – the "lily among the thorns". First, a biblical reference from Song of Songs 2:2. Second, a really obtuse movie reference from *A Knight's Tale* where Paul Bettany refers to himself ... Geoffery Chaucer. I had a very clear technicolor vision of her, the pure white lily, safe and resistant to a world of hurt and danger.

> [NAME redacted but half the people in L.A. probably know who my girlfriend was because I never stopped talking about her]

> *Please do not respond to this email*"

Devastation is mild ... I immediately did what I had promised I would do if we came to any major disagreement. She had expressly asked me not to communicate. Within minutes I was online to my website manager who I told to block incoming e-mails and (to protect myself) to block any outgoing communications. He was told to implement especially rigid content searching from third parties. I also blocked my telephone (in and out). DONE! Huge hole in my heart but I could walk away contending that I had kept my word and followed her directions to the letter – I could be haughtily noble and bitter at the same time!

That I had "over-reacted" would not be my take on the situation regardless of other's perceptions.

For a second time in two days I contacted my existential guru and friend in New Mexico and instead of spin what I said, what I sent her is reproduced below with names redacted:

> **Sent:** Sunday, October 4, 2015 5:33 PM
> **Subject:** [redacted]
>
> Believe it or not that was probably my second psychotic break ever! I can't apologize – you are the only one I know who could possibly understand.
>
> Thank you so much for helping to press the reset button in my tiny brain.
>
> I have always preferred an exceptionally difficult problem in quantum mechanics or integrated field theory to dealing with the infinitely complicated twists and turns of peoples' emotions (self included).
>
> Part of what you heard is my absolute incredulity at how stupid I am and can be regarding what people think and want. It seems I have an almost flat learning curve. Very embarrassing and inconvenient especially when you have to find some popularly acceptable reason for the way you behave.
>
> BACKSTORY – One week ago Duane – silly romantic – was hopelessly engaged in the notion of being in love with someone he had slept with one night 40 years ago. He was a complete jerk and ran away then because he had been in very deep love with someone 4 years before who had begged him to go away with her and she then died in a motorcycle accident that he always felt he should have been in with her. Strange and semi-cosmic details aside, the elation of talking to this 40-year-old connection became hoped-for love, openly sexual repartee then despair when Duane became "too much". Was sending her flowers without seeing her "too much"? The only message on the card was, "You! – Lilium Inter Spinas" ... is that wrong or offensive? Obviously, I did not think so. I am left with pondering how stupid I must be but not having any notion of how to fix it.

I was totally flabbergasted and tried desperately to understand what she meant. How could I be too much? I am only 5'2", medium build, limp, questionable ethnic origin, less than inspiring academic background and numerous other freely admitted flaws – hardly a "too much" profile.

You have unquestionably better judgement than anyone I have ever known. Is being brutally honest about me "too much"? No pressure for you, I just expect a definitive answer within 24 hours.

Love you – and I will totally understand if you WISELY CHOOSE not to respond.

Needless to say, I am now much calmer but still totally perplexed.

Thank you for being you!

D

The response was measured and comforting even though I was not in a particularly receptive state for comforting. My return message to her was:

"**Sent:** Monday, October 5, 2015 10:53 AM
Subject: RE: [redacted]

[redacted]:

I was absolutely correct about you being the wisest person I know. It is very apparent that you have sailed on perilous existential seas, perhaps more than most, and have somehow navigated and kept your sanity. I have read and will try to fully integrate what you said. I have also listened to another very wise woman:

"The cure for anything is salt water: sweat, tears or the sea." [done all 3, multiple times, very recently]

"Difficult times have helped me to understand better than before, how infinitely rich and beautiful life is in every way, and that so many things that one goes worrying about are of no importance whatsoever."
- Isak Dinesen, Danish Writer, April 17, 1885 - September 7, 1962

I actually have a "Man-up" data file of quotations that I need to use more often than I would ever admit to anyone else.

On the issue of beating up on oneself. I never thought of it that way. Maybe it is the cause / effect training. I assume that when something goes wrong it is often my fault and I have been in relationships where it has always been my fault. Therefore, I don't waste much time looking elsewhere; I just scramble to understand the problem and fix whatever failed if at all possible. It is just so much harder when it is me. You are also absolutely right about playing the character, I have never been able to keep it up.

Ah – *"lilium inter spinas"* – the "lily among the thorns". First, a biblical reference from Song of Songs 2:2. Second, a really obtuse movie reference from *A Knight's Tale* where Paul Bettany refers to himself ... Geoffery Chaucer. I had a very clear technicolor vision of her, the pure white lily, safe and resistant to a world of hurt and danger.

> I am almost back to normal because the tragi-comic movie that I carry in my head is now accessible for editing. It is now possible to jump-cut the latest scene with a new version…She was so upset and angry at me for running away after a night of ecstasy and hope for love, that she held a 40-year grudge and delivered the punishment I so richly deserved by rejecting my most ardent and awkward advances… This reads so much better, dramatic irony and poetic justice in one quick scene. It also works so much better as a salve for a bruised ego – that I was worth 40 years of vengeance is much better than not being worth the effort.
>
> Love you [redacted]
>
> … deepest thanks. D
>
> I owe you at least one very good bottle of wine for the unscheduled therapy. The problem is that you will have to share it with me."

My existential guru – a cross between Spinoza and Kant on steroids! A most formidable weapon in a cruel metaphysical universe. She has saved me from the event horizon of the accretion disk more than once.

As in all things there is what really happened and … what people imagined or feared had happened. Fortunately, or unfortunately, the situation is not nearly as epic or clear as anyone would have projected. Reality is often messy, complex and not easily resolved by wishes or slight-of-hand.

What actually happened is not exceptionally clear to me since I went off the deep end but in a lame attempt to be 'fair and balanced' in my reporting I will say that her brother had just died and that the flowers were not going to be taken as a symbol of love but as sympathy that she definitively did not want. Of course, I wanted the flowers to be taken as a symbol of poetic and aspiring love for her. OOPS!

My sister was a key element in reconnecting us. She sent me an e-mail with a word attachment that was immediately picked up by the website e-mail filter. My website manager and I had an agreement that I would not get access to material deemed damaging to me … therefore I did not know exactly what was sent but I did suspect who sent it. This sparked a warning to my sister that sending me "3rd party restricted materials" was potentially dangerous for her e-mail or website because it could initiate an automatic DDoS[18] defensive attack. It was not difficult to surmise who was trying to contact me but I had another problem … I had deliberately cut myself off with software that is not commonly available. I ended up having to go to the local Sprint offices and using their computer directly to unblock my phone. They weren't smart enough to know!

---

[18] DDoS is an acronym for a group of Denial of Service cyberattacks now becoming much more common.

After a few hours of delicate negotiation as to who had overreacted ... we got back together. I still contend that I LITERALLY followed her instructions to the letter but it is clear (in her mind) that I was wrong ... YES DEAR, was my only pathetic response.

Do I love her despite all of the ups and downs? ... Yes.

I had previously written this note when we were still together (June 2016). Although I was still very much in love I had to retire from the field of conflict permanently. As the singer, Pat Benatar, has so effectively said "Love is a Battlefield".[19] Perhaps I was never properly equipped. I hate feeling hurt and being unable to change the situation. I am who I am ... warts and all. I was 63 and it would be foolish to say I will never fall in love again. I had said that before this happened and I was wrong then.

The only thing I can say is that love is wonderful when it works and if it does come along again I will have to be much more cautious and circumspect. I would love to be in love with someone who really loved me and did not view me as a make work project, an odd curio, a cheap fixer-upper, or something that should blend in with the décor. Perhaps a better analysis of the problem with me is that initially women seem to see me as an adorable puppy – in need of training – but adorable. After they have me for a while and find out that I am not easy to house train, make heel, or get past the perfunctory "yes dear" I become an annoying burden. If they wanted a pet they should have been thinking of me more like a cat than dog!

I certainly must give snaps to my two ex-wives for having the balls and lack of real sense to take me home and present me to their parents. That must have been exceptionally difficult! Belated thanks go out to both of you.

Honesty requires that I stipulate that blending in has never been a strong point for me. I am direct, a terrible tease, brutally honest (when not in the tease mode), and literal. Not good defenses in a world where truth is relatively unimportant and impression seems to rule the day. None of us can afford to be the impressions of ourselves or characters in our own bad movie ... it is just simply hard enough to be ourselves.

---

[19] Pat Benatar – "Love is a Battlefield" , . https://www.youtube.com/watch?v=CjY_uSSncQw. Retrieved 07/18/2016.

NOTE 26 – WHAT THAT GUY NEEDS IS A GOOD RAP ON THE HEAD

This is a story about a hospital stay that, by necessity, starts in a rather sketchy manner. The reason for this is a couple of skull fractures, a fractured hip, and some undetermined time being unconscious. But, in my defense, it was not a self-inflicted wound like smashing my foot into a wall on my bike.

I had designed a lifting frame and had it welded together by a welder who I had not used before. It was rather large and was sitting on a concrete pad in my back yard. I was inspecting it before preparing to move it down the driveway for pick-up. This required a ladder and I also had asked my children to give me a hand by putting moving carts under it after I had looked at everything and jacked it up. I climbed up top and distinctly remembered my daughter telling me to be careful. My reply was that although I was carrying a few extra pounds it was insignificant given the strength of the piece … WRONG! Shortly after I said this I do remember looking skyward as I fell backwards towards the ground about 10 feet down. I also knew that my trailing foot was caught in the ladder as an entire section of the structure collapsed.

Well – that is all I remember until about 3 days later. The next part of what I will relate below is reportage from my daughter and son who were immediately at the scene. From their reports, I behaved in a characteristically annoying manner when I was badgered by repeated questions that I found to be foolish.

Apparently, I had fallen on the back and left side of my head before the rest of my body followed and there was blood beginning to come out of my left ear. My daughter had the common sense to call for an ambulance while I was unconscious for several minutes. When I woke up I was apparently as communicative as ever and insisted on trying to get up to continue my inspection. She apparently had little or no trouble holding me down while she insisted that I did not move.

The paramedic team arrived and started checking vital signs and began with a barrage of questions. When asked what my name was I told them, "It's the same as her's." They then asked the address and I apparently said, "Surely you must know the address you got here didn't you?"

At this point my daughter intervened and very firmly told me to stop jerking around and answer the questions that I was being asked. I did manage to give 2 of the 4 digits of the house number but I drew a blank on the street. They then asked where it hurt and my response was "I don't know until I get up but I sure you will tell me". This got an instant rebuke from my daughter and I muttered a few complaints. The paramedics punctured my arm for an IV and proceeded to feel me up like some sex-starved teenagers. I was then strapped to a board and carted away – likely a punishment for my insolence.

As I said earlier, I am only reporting what I was told occurred because my only firm recollection after flying through the air was waking up in the hospital with an incredible headache and an acute desire to pee. I couldn't move because someone had decided I was some kind of "flight risk" and tied me to the bed. I looked around and encompassed that I had done something reasonably dumb and that would account for having IV's in both arms. I will certainly credit the staff with attentive service because I didn't even have the chance to call anyone or find the buzzer – a nurse appeared at my side and asked me how I was. Clearly, I had taken none of my daughter's subconscious admonitions to heart because I said (this I can now relate for myself), "Great, I think I'll just get up and go down to the pub for a nice drink! Would you kindly release me unless I am under arrest for something."

She paused and then said, "Excuse me if I am not entirely sure but that must be the most sensible thing that you have said in a couple of days."

The irresistible opening was presented ... "You listened to me for a couple of days? You really have to get a life!"

She laughed and said, "Glad to see that you will live".

"Isn't that a bit dramatic? I just had a bit of a fall".

She just shook her head and then started with 'THE PEN'. "Please look at the end of the pen and follow it with your eyes and without moving your head".

Since I had not had the time to try out my head and it was hurting like crazy I was happy to oblige and follow the damn pen. I then said, "Could I either have a double vodka with a twist of lime or something else for my headache before my head explodes?" She smiled and told me she would be right back. As she was leaving I added that my bladder would do the same thing if I couldn't pee.

She told me to go ahead and pee whenever I wanted ... it dawned on me that they must have catheterized me. So how do I spell relief "SSSSSSSSSSSSSSSSSSSSSSSSSSSSSSSSSSSS...aaaaaaaaahhh!!"

She returned very quickly and had some young resident in tow. He was affable enough and took the full second it took to introduced himself but immediately reached for the pen and I had to follow it. He then basically related to me what I had already told the nurse ... I had a huge headache. "Would you like something for the pain?"

"No I think I will just lie here and watch the contents of my brain splatter on the ceiling just before I die!" Not a nice response but I have never liked stupid questions. Just as I answered him my monitor went off and both of them got very attentive. Within a few seconds, he reached to one of the IV bags and squeezed it. Within another few seconds I was not longer awake or aware of being awake. I felt that my response to him wasn't impertinent enough to merit knocking me out.

Later (I don't know how much later) I awoke to the same diminutive charge nurse and the first thing I asked was "Does the resident always knock out sassy patients". She smiled and then it finally occurred to me to ask where I was. It turned out to be the ICU unit at UCLA Hospital. She then told me that my intercranial pressure had risen very quickly. I volunteered that it always happened when people asked me stupid questions.

"Well I certainly won't make that mistake so I will bring in your family whether you like it or not! But before that you will have to turn over to your right side for a few seconds." Without even asking she moved around and helped me with a hip and within a few more seconds lifted my gown, whacked my ass sharply and stuck me with a syringe.

"What the hell did I do this time? I hope you are not putting me under again."

"No, that's warfarin, an anticoagulant, and it will be my pleasure to administer it often over the next couple of days."

My family was ushered in and I had the very distinct impression that I had magically risen from the dead. They seemed somewhat pleased to see me (something I am not commonly accustomed to). They all recounted their concerns that I could have died and I assured them that it could not have been that bad. I just hit my head.

I had probably not even asked any of the hospital staff what damages I had incurred and my wife then told me that I had multiple skull fractures, was bleeding out of my left ear and was a complete pain in the ass for the paramedics who came to whisk me away. Rila, my daughter, who was only 14 at the time and who had acquitted herself very well during the incident started asking me all kinds of questions to test my memory. I restrained myself from teasing and apparently passed the test. My only comment was "Sorry to disappoint you all but it is highly likely that a hell of a hit in the head did nothing positive to change my personality".

Over the next couple of days, I began to feel very well indeed and asked if I could get up and go to the washroom. To my surprise the nurse said OK and disconnected my last IV. She proceeded to help me out of bed. I assured her that it was unnecessary but she fortunately insisted because as soon as my right leg had any weight on put on it my hip hurt like hell and I asked her to let me sit down in a chair … that also hurt. She did not hesitate for a second and immediately asked how long it had been bothering me. I told her very honestly that my hip had been a bit of a problem all of my life but I really wasn't joking about it hurting. Within 5 minutes the orthopedic resident for ICU was in the room and asking me to walk. Without getting up I told him that would be a complete waste of time since I had a very pronounced limp ever since I started walking (many years before). I told him I had polio and it seemed to ignite a small response in his right cortex. I volunteered that I probably damaged it when I fell and was unsure whether the paramedics checked it because it was highly unlikely that I was cooperative or helpful at that time – besides, I didn't remember a thing.

Within 30 minutes I was inside the MRI tunnel and getting a lower body scan. Big surprise!?? I had a fractured hip. I had to wait a few hours for the orthopedic surgeon and he was surprisingly experienced and candid. He said that my scans were very "interesting" and that there was no point in trying to do anything since I didn't put a lot of my weight on that side anyway. He also said that he would prescribe as much painkiller as I would need for at least one month until it mended itself. He actually asked if that was OK with me and I responded with my own catch phrase, "Better living through chemistry". He smiled knowledgably and that was it.

The next morning my favorite nurse came in to tell me that the chief of neurology was coming by with his students. Within 30 seconds it was abundantly clear that he was the typical self-important egomaniac who needed an audience, preferably as silent as possible, in order to feel all the more important. After several days of being in the ICU my boredom levels had reached epic proportions so when I saw him rounding the corner into my room with a flotilla of residents I could not help myself in taking advantage of a person so clearly without a sense of humor or any real imagination.

Without even saying hello or good morning or how's it hangin?, he pulled out a pen from his pristine white lab coat (clearly not one in which any useful work ever got done) and began to wave it in my face like a boy scout practicing to get a merit badge in semaphore. He proceeded with a ritual that I had been through virtually every hour for days. "Look at the tip of my pen and follow it".

He was very rude in not asking please and he clearly had no concern that I really didn't feel like doing it. I had never been good at imitating a trained seal and was loath to do it for someone with an unwilling "posse". As he moved the pen to the right I moved my eyes in the opposite direction. The same for every movement. After a few of these he began pouring over my chart. My favorite charge nurse (maybe 4' 10") was standing between two towering residents and very clearly stifling a giggle. She was giving me the "no" indication with a shaking head and all I did was smile. The residents began to jostle amongst each other and make furtive asides but a couple of them dared to smile a bit as well.

The boss decided that they would convene to a conference room around the corner and as soon as they started to leave she came over to me and punched the poor delicate patient in the shoulder. She told me that she was not very pleased that I had forced her into going into the conference room and revealing that I had the intrinsic personality flaw (or mental deficit) of teasing people. She told me that the alternative was that she could leave him perplexed and ordering an entire battery of tests to cover his sorry ass (she didn't add that, I did). Needless-to-say, he did not ever return to make a display of examining one of his patients in public. There was no time wasted in dealing any further with me. He signed his consent to release me that afternoon.

NOTE 27 – MY BEST BIRTHDAY EVER

After 25 years of marriage I got divorced in February of 2015. It was as amicable as anyone could have wanted and my ex was magnanimous in letting me stay on until I had a better idea of what I might do with my life.

My 62nd birthday was rapidly approaching is September and I decided that I wanted to go to Chile. I offered my ex and my children the opportunity to come with me. My daughter, who has routinely said to me "Dad … you didn't think it through did you?", decided to question my "thinking" or at least my intent. Her first question was "What is so interesting about Chile?"

"Wine, grapes, the Andes, and the Atacama Desert."

She then very firmly said, "Really Dad, what do you want to see in Chile?"

My slow and honest response was, "The ESO [European Southern Observatories] runs the three best observatories there."

Her response was visually graphically clear, a pronounced thumb down with the auditory accompaniment of the Rila buzzer "ZZZZZZZZZZ".

It was abundantly clear that I would be alone and I was ecstatic. It was totally selfish and it was the first time in 25 years that I had allowed myself to feel that way let alone enjoy it.

The only real preparations that I did were to make appointments at the observatories and then try to figure out the driving plan to get to them. They were La Silla, home of the HARPS (**H**yper **A**ccurate **R**adial velocity **P**lanet **S**urvey) and Paranal (primarily a fabulous optical array telescope) both in the lower Atacama Desert, and ALMA (a very large radio telescope array) in the far north.

The balance of my pseudo-plan was to get to Valparaíso, an historic gritty port city at some time during the trip and to drive to the end of the Pan-America Highway at Puerto Montt. In Puerto Montt my hotel room was on the top floor and the balcony looked south and west. The almost exact location was 41°28'24.8"S 72°56'07.3"W. The key element in looking west from Puerto Montt is that there is virtually no land mass between 40 to 50 south to moderate the winds in any way.

There was no better illustration of this than when I walked out of the south facing doors on the balcony and turned the corner to look westward. I was literally pushed back by wind that must have been in the range of 35-40 miles per hour out of the west. It was like hitting a wall. I spoke to some locals later and commented on the wind and two of them laughed and added that it was a reasonably mild day!

It was very beautiful. Looking toward the south all I could see were islands. Everything south of Puerto Montt is punctuated by fjords and the only ways to get there are by boat or to drive around into Argentina to go to the southernmost 1/3 of Chile down to the very base of South America – Tierra de Fuego (the Land of Fire). As a testament to my lack of thinking things through, I had not really considered the large amount of additional time that it would take to get there. Cape Horn (the southern-most tip of Chile is at 55°40'30.7"S 68°04'26.5"W. The distance from Puerto Montt to Cape Horn is approximately 1,664 km (1,034 mi) by air almost due south. This would be much longer if you had to drive and you really can't drive to the tip at Cape Horn anyway. The closest you could get by car would probably be Ushuaia, Argentina (2482 km, 1542 mi) and that is still far short of Cape Horn.

Chile is incredibly long and narrow. "Chile has an extreme north-south length of **approximately 4,300 kilometres (about 2,672 miles)**, but its average width is less than **180 kilometres** (less than **112 miles**), and nowhere is it more than **356 kilometres** (221 miles) wide."[20] I drove from Puerto Montt in the south to Antofagasta in the north (still short of all of the way north – by 719 km to Arica near the Peruvian border) and managed to cover 2,366 km (1470 mi).

My first observatory visit was at La Silla in the lower Atacama Desert, one of the driest places in the world. It had not rained at that site in 12 years but as I started down the several-kilometer dirt road leading to both it and the Las Campanas Observatory it began to rain and at times it was a very strong downpour. I thought little of this as it seems to be typical thunderstorms that were in intermittent cells. As I watched drops ricochet off the hard ground I decided that since there were clearly no cops or traffic, I would have some fun so I chose a really flat off-road patch and started doing donuts and figure eights with the car. The wet clay acted like ice and it reminded me of my first car in a Canadian winter. After I got a bit dizzy and bored I continued on so that I would not be late. The ESO e-mail said that if you were not at the security gates on time you would not be admitted at all. This would be more than a little inconvenient since I wasin the middle of nowhere in a rainy desert with little or no apparent help available.

---

[20] https://www.google.com/?ion=1&espv=2#q=lenght%20and%20width%20of%20chile

Within a couple of kilometers of the gate it was strange to find a very well kept paved road. It was very clear that it was European money and not Chilean that had built the road and the rather flashy security checkpoint. I drove right up to the gate and there was only one other car. I was twenty minutes early so I pulled to the side under a tree and poured myself a congratulatory glass of wine.

After the twenty minutes the people in the other car walked to the gate and tried to get the security guard to come out to speak to them. I then walked up and after some pretty emphatic waving we coaxed him to come out of the building to the gate. We all had our invitations and ID ready but he would not open the gate and then beginning speaking very quickly in Spanish. I understood only about half of what he was saying and it was absolutely clear that the other two people understood substantially less.

I managed to ask the guard to slow down. He told me that we could not go up because of snow. The people from the other car then turned to me for translation (a very bad idea given my poor Spanish). I then tried to get an estimate of how long it would be before we could go up. He did not hesitate for a second and told me two days. At this point the other people decided that we would speak in English because they were from Sweden. I immediately apologized and told them the news. They volunteered that they had extended their trip to Brazil to come and see their nephew who was a visiting scientist at the observatory. They did not know what to do so I asked the guard if we could use his phone to call up top so that they could talk to him. Initially he did not respond but I stumbled through their sad story and kept on about how they needed to speak with him so he handed over the phone and after a few minutes talking with him they explained that he was heartbroken but it would probably be two days and it was not safe for him to come down in the present storm. The poor family were only 5000 or 6000 feet apart but it was really half of the world at this point.

They did not know what to do with the gift and bottle of wine that they had brought for him. I was also initially very disappointed that I could not go up but I quickly became embarrassed by my singular selfishness. In order to make myself feel less unworthy I decided that since the guard seemed particularly malleable I would try to do one productive thing. I told them to write a note on the wine and present and I would make the guard responsible to take them up to him when possible. After a lot of arguing and cajoling the guard took the present and wine through the bars and we got in our cars and sadly left the way we had come.

I had come a very long way to discuss exoplanet research with the people who were actually doing it and as I drove I just couldn't get over the cosmic irony of having a few flakes of snow spoil it. As I drove on I saw the side road for the other observatory. Not willing to completely accept defeat I set out on the mucky road that led to Las Campanas Observatory.[21] There was no gate and I was prepared to give it a try. It was not raining but as I climbed it started to snow, first lightly, then quite steadily. The road was wet and channels of water were flowing downhill past me. After about two kilometers of a very steep and windy climb I got to the ice. The car would not climb another foot on the slick road and after a couple of tries I started to slide backwards with little help from the brakes at all. This was certainly adrenaline producing but I figured that if I slid off the road up here I would be condor carrion before they would ever find me.

I had to go in reverse for about one half kilometer until I had to turn around a second time that day. I was surprisingly sanguine about the whole mess. It was very clear that the accretion disk existed around my existential black hole and I had just escaped being completely pulled into it … like sliding off of the side of a mountain trying to get to an observatory that probably would not have let me in anyway because I had failed to follow "PROCEDURE". As a small consolation, I stopped just before getting onto the highway and I poured myself another glass of wine with which I toasted the cosmos for "its epic cruelty and total lack of concern for such creatures as me".

Independence Day in Chile was September 18. I arranged to be in the capitol but as a pedestrian for the last three days of my trip. I had planned to enjoy the festivities so I wanted to return the car so that my own celebration would not be impaired by events so much as by wine.

When I drove back to the car rental lot at the airport the attendant initially would not lift the gate to let me in and insisted on looking at the rental agreement. It seemed a little strange but all was made clear when he ran a finger across the hood of the car and made a long rut in the very thick crust of grey clay that covered the car except for the windows.

I went into the airport to settle with the rental company and there were several phone calls from the front desk to the lot. My rudimentary Spanish was sufficient for me to understand that the problem that the agent was having was the mileage. I interrupted and asked him why there was a problem. He said that he wanted the lot attendant to check the odometer again because it could not be correct. I then asked him what number he had and he told me 6800 km. I nodded my head and said, "Si, eso est correcto!" He then started to mouth something and I added, "El contacto dijo kilometraje ilimitado.

---

[21] Las Campanas / Carnegie Observatories. "The twin 6.5-meter Magellan telescopes are widely considered to be the best natural imaging telescopes in the world. They were built and continue to be operated by a consortium consisting of the Carnegie Institution of Washington, Harvard University, MIT, the University of Michigan, and the University of Arizona. The telescopes are located at Carnegie's Las Campanas Observatory, high in the southern reaches of Chile's Atacama Desert. First light for the Walter Baade telescope occurred on September 15, 2000. The Landon Clay telescope started science operations on September 7, 2002." http://www.lco.cl/ Retrieved 07/22/2016.

[The contract said unlimited mileage]." He seemed shocked that I had driven 6800 km in about 14 days. It was not nearly enough to properly see Chile but I gave it my best shot!

I got a taxi from the airport to my hostel / hotel in the older part of central Santiago. It was charming and alive with foot traffic and late evening shopping that I thought was clearly in preparation for the Independence celebrations.

Early the next morning I woke up with an urge to prowl the streets and take pictures. Most of the balance of my trip had taken place at a much different scale and pace – driving and consuming the scenes but not really taking their full measure.

I climbed up the large hill, Cerro Santa Lucia, which is a very beautifully terraced park that provides an excellent panoramic view of the city and mountains if you scale it to the summit. It even has a chapel and a castle (Castillo Hidalgo) on its slopes. After a couple of hours I descended onto to streets to capture as many shots as caught my eye as I made my way to the fine arts museum.

Having assaulted myself with art at the Museo Nacional de Bellas Artes, I found myself across the street in the Parque Forestal on the terrace of another historic building. The terrace was a recent addition to an historic building and is part of a fairly up-scale restaurant. All I wanted was a café cortado (like a latte) but I looked at the lunch menu and was unfairly influenced. I ordered a large carafe of a nice dry red wine and sat down to enjoy my three courses that were great but the opener was so unexpected.

Two waiters came proudly to the table with a pile of mushy steaming onions in the bottom of a large martini glass. The lead waiter deposited 4 small white ovoid objects atop the mound. He ceremoniously received a pitcher of hot broth from a groveling intern and poured it over the top. He then covered it with a saucer and asked me to be patient for about 1 minute. I removed the saucer took a picture and then was blown away. The 4 white ovoid objects were miniature scallops. Of course, idiot boy, failed to look at the two shells on the side of the plate that contained a mildly spicy but delicious mayonnaise and grated cheese. Of course, they were scallop shells! Anyway, it was spectacularly delicious. I had not conceived of a **deconstructed French onion soup** – fabulous! Foolish of me not to expect the Spanish to do that to the French.

The next day I had expected to be a very spirited Independence Day but I was very mistaken, and frankly blind-sided by my total lack of political and social intelligence. I did get to see an assembly in the central plaza but there were probably just as many police as there were spectators. I began to cruise the streets and take many pictures of the recent graffiti that told the real story of political and social friction that I had previously missed completely. Despite this or perhaps because of it, in a little over two weeks I learned to love Chile for its variety of climates, constant surprises, lack of llamas, and the affability of the people that I met.

NOTE 28 – BAIKONUR … SCREW THE RUSSIANS

My best birthday ever was followed by my most unexpected birthday ever. After a great trip in Chile I was very soon afterwards planning a bike tour in Kazakhstan, Uzbekistan, and Tajikistan. This was truly an experience on the accretion disk and very much the model of a life that most people would not believe anyway – so what the hell, I tell the story anyway.

I started my plans for a long bike trip by working out every day in the gym. Then, in about June (2015) I got on the Internet and started to look for bicycle clubs in Kazakhstan. This should have been easy but it turned out to be much more difficult than I had anticipated. All I wanted was to find a group that did distance riding – "a social peloton" so-to-speak. After a number of e-mails it turned out that my suggestion of 60-100 miles a day (96.6-151 km; 4 to 5 hours of riding) seemed to be in the realm of crazy; at least for the riders in Astana.

It is hard to deconvolute my thinking for the trip but I do know that one of the components was a strong historic interest in the old silk road and the romantic and exotic names like Samarkand and Tashkent. I could see myself riding into those cities on my tadpole recumbent trike like the wandering Marco Polo on his way to China.

Another very strong desire was to visit Baikonur, the launch site for the USSR and since, for Russia, from everything from Sputnik[22], to Laika[23] the space dog, to Yuri Gagarin[24]. The city of Baikonur is a closed Russian city on the western steppe in a bend of the Syr Darya River that is "rented" from Kazakhstan. It is not overstatement to suggest that this is indeed a very important historic site. The very launch pad that sent Laika into space is named Gagarin's Start (Гагаринский старт : Gagarinskij start).

In a kind of weird synthetic way, I saw the trip as a marriage of two histories - the ancient world and the modern one – space and the silk road – how naively romantic – how unfortunately very much like I am.

---

[22] Sputnik was launched on October 4, 1957. It was an aluminum sphere with 4 radio antennae and it transmitted signals for several weeks until its batteries ran out. These were indeed the beeps that changed the modern world.

[23] Laika, a stray dog from the streets of Moscow was the first living creature to orbit the Earth. She was sent on a non-return trip in Sputnik **2** in November 1957, was said to have died painlessly in orbit about a week after blast-off. This may not be the entire truth of it.

[24] "Yuri Alekseyevich Gagarin was a Russian Soviet pilot and cosmonaut. He was the first human to journey into outer space, when his Vostok spacecraft completed an orbit of the Earth on 12 April 1961." https://en.wikipedia.org/wiki/Yuri_Gagarin. Retrieved 07/25/2016.

The bike trip was really the first part of it that went up in flames, perhaps a fiery crash, or maybe just a sidetrack into the sand in the western Kazak desert. Besides not being able to get any riders who wanted to go on an extended trek from Astana, the capital in the north east, to Baikonur in the south western steppe (about 1234 km or 767 mi). When I am fit, I can do 100 miles per day but at a controlled pace, more tortoise than hare. I was then had to mentally prepare myself to go it alone. That was not too difficult since I really wanted to do it and then continue the bike trip in a circle from Baikonur to Tashkent and on to Samarkand, then Bishkek and back to Astana. The distance would have been 4586 km. There were absolutely no takers – where was Borat when I need him?

My next move was to try to get information about bicycling the route and what amenities I might expect from the Department of Transportation of Kazakhstan. They had never had anyone ask "such a question" and promised to get back to me. They never did even after 1 month and at least ten e-mails from me. The more research and fewer answers that I actually received, the less determined I became about biking so then I acquiesced to a rental car. This also became a very interesting venture.

Baikonur was a completely different problem. I needed a visa since, although it is in Kazakhstan, it is really still Russia and is closed – you need a Russian visa. However, for a sinful amount of money one can get tours of Baikonur originating in Moscow or Astana. These were about the estimated cost of my entire trip and I had no intention of going there for a day with a tour group and being headed by docents (or the equivalent) who would not be prone to answer anything but the most banal questions. As a scientist, I really wanted to talk to scientists.

I again went on line and found that the nearest consular office for the Russian Federation was in San Francisco. After several tries it was impossible to even get on their server. Either travelling to Russia was incredibly popular or IT services in San Francisco were incredibly poor. I then did something almost unheard of and used the phone. I had done a bit of homework first and decided to try to speak to a real person with a name so I asked for the vice-consul and was connected to a secretary who asked who I was. It was clear immediately that I had to make a significant positive impression or I would just be blown off. I told her that I was a scientist who formerly worked in Canada and now lived in the USA and was interested in visiting Russia and some specific scientific sites. She immediately transferred me to her boss who was indeed the vice-consul.

After I explained that I was only bothering him because it was impossible to get through online he said "Da, we often have that problem." We had an initial affable chat and then he proceeded on a more specific line of questions. When he finally got to where I wanted to go and I said Baikonur there was a distinct pause in his generally very smooth and glib delivery. He then pleasantly offered the possibility of joining a tour from Moscow. I said that I had looked into tours and it just was not what I wanted to do. Perhaps I should not have offered the added information (as one of my ex-wives will corroborate) that as I scientist I really wanted to talk to scientists. He then asked for my e-mail and told me that he would be back in touch with me.

This all seemed fine until about three days later I got an e-mail from some aide in the consulate asking me about my scientific background. I thought it was a bit weird but I gave him one of my websites with a downloadable CV. The next day I got another e-mail asking me, "What type of scientist were you?" I thought that a 21-page CV would suffice to answer most questions one might have about my background. I then wrote a very terse reply. "Environmental / Nuclear ... excellent by all reports". Probably not the wisest reply but it seemed like I was dealing with a bit of a dunce if not just a flunky. Another day passed and I was asked specifically about the nuclear work that I did since it was "not really in my vitae." That was incisive and was a correct observation. Much of what I actually did couldnot be published.

I had no problem with my next reply since it had been nearly 30 years since I had work in nuclear so I was brutally honest and told the person that work on nuclear risk assessments and waste disposal issues and most of that was classified but was very unimportant and low-level stuff that any student could have performed. This very honest response brought no reply. I waited for a couple of weeks but the pressure of planning a trip that had not any real plan was getting on my nerves so I sent of a series of e-mails (one per day for at least a week). This did finally get a response but not one I would have ever dreamed.

It was unsigned and simply said "We cannot grant your request for a travel visa to Baikonur at this time. It may be possible to apply for a visa with the approval of the Russian Academy of Sciences... Thank you for your interest in visiting the Russian Federation." WHOA! Talk about getting stiffed... I not only got a refusal I got the flaming red finger. How the hell would a nothing scientist get approval from the Russian Academy let alone WHY? I was extremely vexed but the only thing that I could do at that point was to curse over a couple of large glasses of old vine zin and try to figure out what I did wrong.

Having finished the wine, I immediately got on my computer. I have an old Russian associate in St. Petersburg and I sent him an e-mail explaining the situation and asking for his help with contacts that he might have at Baikonur. This got another strange reply. He did not respond to the e-mail I sent (not my normal one but a new one on g-mail) but instead contacted me through the information link on one of my websites. In addition, the originating ISP was not traceable. He told me I was crazy, gave me 3 contacts, told me that he had repaid any favors that he owed me and, don't contact him for a minimum of couple of years. Keep in mind this is not the cold war it is 2015 (about August) but I felt like I was in some kind of movie like ... *Bridge of Spies*. "Holy crap on a cracker!"[25]

Now I was more intrigued than anything so I did what I always do ... pushed some buttons. I contacted the persons and all of them had the same basic responses ... we don't know who you are, we are sorry we have no useful information, good luck trying to see where Laika (the first space dog) last peed.

---

[25] I have to credit my knowledge and extreme overuse of this phrase to the character of Penny on *Big Bang Theory*. https://www.youtube.com/watch?v=j_Z0kTkFFWc. Retrieved 08/06/2016.

It was exceptionally clear that I would not be getting a visa to visit Baikonur (at least not in my lifetime). There was no way that I would be have another special birthday as I had the previous year in Chile.

A couple of days later I was sitting in the locker room of my local YMCA at 6:45 in the morning and bitching to one of the regulars that the trip I had been so excited about a month before was a bust. My cell phone rang and I looked at it and saw that it was from Texas. I know a couple of people in Texas but I don't know what possessed me to answer, I usually don't even have my phone in the gym, but I answered in a surly manner – "YES!"

The reply was slow, deep and measured "Duane, you have been bad!"

"Who the hell are you?"

"You don't remember?"

"I said who the hell are you? If you are one of my ex-students I will tell you that you chose an incredibly bad time to be yanking my chain."

"Now don't be so upset; you clearly don't remember that you turned down a job with us a couple of years ago." I had not been looking for a job but I did remember a discussion with someone from Homeland Security about the possibility of me working on a project to look at how art theft and transfers of art might be a revenue source for terrorism. My immediate reaction was that it was really a no-brainer, a poor cash flow for terrorists, and I was not remotely interested. At this point I said:

"There is no way you are from Homeland Security and if you are then who are you."

"I really can't say".

"Then I really don't want to talk to you!"

Before I could hang up he interjected a very rapid question "Maybe you could tell me why you have looked up nuclear reactors more than 450 times in the last two months?"

Holy crap on a cracker. "So, you are from homeland and you do have a file on me!"

"I couldn't say".

"You can't or you won't or both?" No response. "If you actually are even half good at intelligence work you would know I am writing a book on climate change and that is just part of the research I have been doing."

"Very nice title *The Nuclear Family: Aggressive Solution for Climate Change*, perhaps a little bit of a red flag in the wrong circles don't you think?"

"Anybody could know that – I just managed to have one of the most unsuccessful appeals for financial support for that book on KICKSTARTER – not a dollar, even from relatives – 0! So, you do have a file on me!"

"I can assure you that you are of no direct importance to us but anyone who looks up nuclear a few hundred times in short succession must assume that it will attract some interest in responsive organizations. As a scientist, it should not be too difficult for you to figure out that the Russians would indeed be very interested in you – I am sure you that you know they launched nuclear platforms into space from there."

"You know this for a fact?"

"They do seem determined to find out why you are so interested in talking to scientists at Baikonur."

Now I was just plain pissed off ... "Fucking Russians, all I wanted to do was to go to an historic site, see where Laika peed, Yuri blasted off from and find out about their present programs and other cool stuff!"

"I can assure you that if we did have a file on you, the Russians' would be very much larger at this point. It may be wise to plan your next trip outside of former Soviet territories. Goodbye".

I sat there partially dressed for a workout and did not know what to say to anyone. I closed my phone, skipped my normal workout and left – SCREW THE RUSSIANS FOR SCREWING UP MY BIRTHDAY PLANS.

NOTE 29 – ROBERTO AND THE PIRANHA

My eight-year-old daughter wanted a piranha for Christmas (2001) and I said that I would get her one – after all, isn't that what fathers do? Besides, this was so much better than Barbies (something she had dispensed with).

I was incredibly naïve and had not realized that it was illegal to sell or own them in California. This, in no way, discouraged a local aquarium shop from accommodating the request but in a very amusing and quasi-surreptitious manner. The first encounter with the shop resulted in an initial deliberate misdirection. Since the couldn't sell me a piranha (they did not tell me why) they said that they could get me a pacu instead. Apparently, it is an omnivorous substitute for an actual piranha with the rather creepy trait of having very human-like teeth. I was sure that I could not pass off a pacu as a piranha, at least where my daughter was concerned. I knew her well enough to know that she would be looking for pointy, razor-sharp teeth, the correct coloring and other ephemera,

The entire charade was more than a bit comic. I had to say loudly and with felling that I really wanted a pacu (nudge-nudge wink-wink). I was then told that they didn't have any in the store but they would get me one within a few days. In the interim I could make sure that the aquarium was ready and at the correct temperature because they are warm water fish. The price was agreed upon in advance but I would have to pick up the fish at a yet undisclosed location when I got a phone call. Normally I would have never agreed bit this was just too precious to pass up. Somehow, I envisioned knocking on some back door in an alley and have to say, to a huge bouncer, … "Bruno sent me for the scaly one!"

In a couple of days I got the call and proceeded to a different aquarium store and I went to the back door – as instructed. I was duly identified and handed a 5-gallon pail two-thirds filled with water, weeds and what I was supposed to take on face value was the piranha disguised as a pacu. I proceeded home and with my daughter's gleeful assistance we poured the contents into the aquarium. There was indeed a small but very easily identifiable red bellied piranha (genus pygocentrus)[26] who immediately disappeared into rocks placed in the corner. It was a beautiful fish if one really had the time to observe. Rila and I then proceed to the aquarium store to make sure that we had everything.

Of course, the aquarium store was pleased that we had a piranha because they were guaranteed a steady market for "feeder fish" – nice live tidbits for our friend. We got at least 50 of them. Of course, we had not done any real research on what actual piranha eating habits were but buying a bunch of food is never wrong if your guests happen to be hungry.

---

[26]The red bellied piranha is one of the most widespread species, and is found in rivers in southern and central South America. I found this out somewhere several years ago and was too lazy to cross-check it.

After dumping the live food into the tank my daughter was expecting some kind of feeding frenzy like on the animal action shows. Even though I had also seen them I assured her that the fish was probably more than a bit in shock having been in one tank, a 5-gallon bucket, a new tank and having been through a rain of new fish. I told her she would have to be patient before she saw what she really wanted … CARNAGE!

With the brief respite, I thought that maybe I should do a little research and most of it was material that Rila would really not want to hear. In general, piranhas are dark water fish, which means they live in muddy water and seem to be somewhat uncomfortable with clear, well-lit areas. One of the people at the aquarium store gave use some dye to put into the water to make it darker and murkier. I had no idea whether this was based on actual research but it sounded good and it fit in very well with our predispositions for the macabre.

After about a week of obsessive observation I was greeted in the livening room at an uncharacteristically early hour for my daughter who happily reported "a kill" … well only a partial kill. She was delighted to see one of the feeder fish basically severed in half and making gasping circles at the top of the water. There was a perfect arc of teeth marks right across the body. She would have been much happier if she had witnessed the grizzly deed but it was clear that this particular piranha was either nocturnal or very, very shy. This seemed highly inconsistent with the reported ferocity of the species or perhaps highly consistent with peoples' tendency to exaggerate.

After a couple of more weeks and a constant disappearance of fish it was clear that the piranha had a good appetite but did not like to dine while anybody was watching. Rila's interest rapidly waned other than having bragging rights to owning a piranha and telling her friends how dangerous it could be if you put your hand into the tank – hence the origin of urban myths like microwaving your dog to dry its fur.

However, in one of our lots of feeder fish there was an unexpected guest – a fair sized crayfish. This was a great addition to the tank and I convinced Raef (Rila's younger brother – about 5 at the time) that the crayfish was his and he could name him. Without any hesitation Raef named the crayfish "Robbie". That, was likely the shortest lasting name for a crayfish ever bestowed. The reason was that Rila immediately took her place as older sister and told Raef that Robbie was not a masculine enough name and she summarily decided that the crayfish would be "Roberto…" Although I failed to grasp the change completely, Roberto was a little more catching and somewhat more like a Latin lover or a swashbuckler.

Roberto was very much more interesting than the piranha. He immediately took up residence behind a single rock in the opposite corner of the aquarium from the "hide" that I had created to allow the piranha some cover. Over the next week he developed a strong sense of territory and would swipe at the passing piranha with his pincers as he stood atop his rock. He was clearly feisty as hell and the piranha learned to give him a decently wide berth. In addition to being aggressive with the piranha Roberto developed a most amusing habit. He would grab feeder fish, munch off their fins ad stack them in the corner behind his rock. It was the strangest thing! He had created a live fish pantry. There were always at least two in the pile and I saw as many as five. He grew very quickly as the proprietor of a fish drive in (but none drove out). I tried to research such behavior but with no success.

One day I noticed that Roberto seemed to be struggling and then I quickly realized that he was molting and trying to crawl out of his now undersized exoskeleton. This was fascinating for everyone and I held back my normal tendency to point out the potential difficulties with the scenario. Raef was particularly interested in the new and bigger Roberto that was imminent.

The next morning I woke up a bit late and to an unusual chorus of tears from the living room, Raef was crying by the aquarium and Rila was offering the barest modicum of sisterly support. They were looking at the discarded carapace and it was clear that there were bits of crayfish floating about the tank. Apparently the piranha decided to have a late evening lobster dinner! She turned to me with no attempt to disguise her glee with the outcome of the encounter. This brought more tears from Raef and she told him it was perfectly natural that Roberto would die without protection. As I said, the barest modicum of sisterly support. Perhaps none of us can really change our skins.

NOTE 30 – INTERNATIONAL TALK LIKE A PIRATE DAY

My favorite date of the year is September 19. It beats X-mas, July 4, Tet, and any other possible holiday hands down! International Talk Like a Pirate Day encapsulates the fantasies or aspirations of most people, be they men or women. From Errol Flynn as Captain Blood, Johnny Depp as Captain Jack Sparrow, or Tim Curry as Long John Silver there is a remarkable charisma and romanticism attached to pirates.

More to the point, no one really wants to work in their dull nine-to-five job and have to go back home to the same bitchy/whiney mate (male or female) every night only to dream of adventures, booty and booties on the high seas and in every pirate port from Zanzibar to Tortuga. ARRRR … who would not want to "keelhaul" people who irritate you? I have a raft of relatives that I would gladly make walk the plank in shark infested waters. My apology to the sharks is explicitly given.

Other incredible selling points for this as a truly fabulous day are:

- The ability to drink as much grog (or anything you please) with no apology because that is what you are expected to do!
- Total selfishness in terms of selected amusements.
- Lack of any necessity to buy a present for anyone but yourself … arrrr just take anything you want!
- Freedom from politicians (and government). "Hang'em all from the yardarm!"
- No need to shave (men nor women).
- Floggings for all telemarketers …

The list could go on but it is abundantly clear that many people have mis-chosen their favorite holidays, or feast days.

When I first discovered the kindred pirate spirits around the world I immediately adopted the day as my own and got a bit carried away trying to convert random people on the street to the ways of piracy. This was a lot like the Jesuit missionaries in the new world trying to convert unwilling natives who eventually showed their lethal displeasure.

On the September 19th itself I adopted a very colorful bandana and then I made a real leather eye patch. I tied up my pants with another piece of colorful rag and then I remembered a large wooden parrot earring that I bought to celebrate my first divorce. It was perfectly battered and a proper ornamentation for a pirate. It was very lucky that I live on the accretion disk because I was already blessed with a rather distinctive limp that I had from when I could walk. So… pirate with a good limp (no cheesy peg leg), parrot earring, and eyepatch. All I was missing was a good cutlass and knife for my belt. There is really no substitute for a cutlass since it was a short rugged sword good in close quarters like boarding and strong enough to slash through rigging. For my first attempt at being a pirate I had to settle for an epee from my former days as a competitive fencer. It was a bit too frou-frou for a real pirate but it had to do.

I was so into being the pirate I just went about my normal business that day which included picking up both of my kids from gymnastics. When I got to the gym I put on my eye patch and immediately caught all of the rhythmic gymnastics girls in a huddle on the mat instead of working. It was clear that their emaciated Russian coach, Olga, was out in the parking lot snagging a cigarette. So I slipped off my shoes, walked out onto the mat flailing the air with my epee and screamed in my best pirate voice, "AVAST you shiftless wenches! Get back to yer exercises or I will have ya flogged and keel hauled! ARRRR. Rila … you be walkin' the plank the next time I see ya lollygaggin."

This got some tittering from the girls who ran in every direction. The only one who stood there fastly was my daughter who did not need a cutlass because she was giving me the dagger eyes and she emanated her seething desire to have a more explicable father. I think I could have taken her in a duel but the gym might not have approved of a battle to first blood.

I went to the other side of the gym to hone my verbal abuse on the boy's team. They seemed to have been enjoying the effect on the girls and as I came over I got some collegial "Arrrrs". However, my son could be seen escaping to the high bar which would provide him some natural protection and distance from the approaching pirate raid. Had he not been so young he might have even been seeking enough distance to claim a level of credible deniability. He too was not going to admit that I was his father despite that fact that I am confident everyone actually knew.

I encourage everyone of sound mind to abandon their birthdays and accept International Talk Like a Pirate Day (September 19th)[27] as their own special celebration!

---

[27] http://talklikeapirate.com/wordpress/ … Arrrr … for many details!

NOTE 31 – WHAT I DON'T GET - BILLION DOLLAR DEAD HAIR

At the gym one morning Daniel (who really has no hair to speak of) complained that he left his shampoo and conditioner at home. This comment turned more than one head. Instead of making one of my more smart-ass comments I reached into my bag and offered him my shampoo. He rejected the gesture immediately and then I had no reason to restrain my responses to the inane and pointless whining of a guy with no hair to speak of.

"What … do you think that it was too cruel to crush up all of the baby argans to make the argan oil for the conditioner?"

At this point, our resident fact-checker, morality monitor and philosopher, AJ, pointed out that argan oil came from the buds or nuts on trees in Morocco. I told him to be quiet because he was spoiling my delivery of the bait. Besides, "It doesn't matter what you use on your hair it's dead keratin … the protein doesn't give a crap."

AJ again interjected with something about nutrients for the hair. I repeated in an even louder voice directed at him. "It's dead JIM! It's dead… it doesn't require nutrients. Split will do as well as with axle grease, Vaseline or Brylcreem".

AJ then retorted, "Are you saying that a billion dollar industry is wrong?"

"DUH… YES!"

James, our resident Greek-American economist, remarked that he loved the gym in the morning due to the tenor of the conversation. A bit facetious but right on point.

It is definitely NOT EXTREME to suggest that MOST ADVERTISING (AT LEAST FOR COSMETICS) IS BULLSHIT. Most of the products are just modified war paint or decoration for tribal rituals. At a minimum one would be very hard pressed to prove what the manufacturers are claiming is true or not true. Many advertisers spend more on lawyers to protect themselves from false claims than they do on actually developing products that work as claimed. All anyone has to do is look at the fine print on most labelling or hidden deep within a website. They are crooks and we are dupes (the people too stupid to say no just in case logic and common sense really don't exist)!

NOTE 32 – "IRONIC" HIPSTER

OK – June 2016, man bun, shaved sides of head, beard (had it "since I was 3"), one week's facial hair, and 63 years old. I am an aging wannabe hipster who is probably 5 years behind the curve. Not bad since I generally don't begin to like anything or doing anything until almost everyone else doesn't anymore or doesn't even remember what the look was or what I am talking about.

I can't quite put my finger on it. Am I just being non-conformist to be different? NO. Do I not really get it at the time. I honestly don't really know. There is certainly a strong Groucho Marx component in my own behavior in that "I don't want to belong to any club that will accept people like me as a member"[28]. Groups of people who surround themselves with other people who think and act exactly like them make me very nervous – whether it is the KKK, the Black Panther's, or ISIS, conformism to narrow concepts or rules can be extremely dangerous.

Having said the above it is highly likely that I am really covering for the fact that I generally pay little attention to what fashion trends exist and what people do on a day to day basis usually passes right under my radar.

So why the belated conversion to a man-bun, dude-bun … whatever? For me, it actually looks OK and hides some very obvious deficiencies that my ex-girlfriend helpfully pointed out like thinning hair on my crown that she not-so-delicately called a "monkey-face".

The real reason is that I needed a change of look to go with my change of life that started two years ago and hair choice was better than many others things and certainly easy enough to implement relative to personality modifications. When I look in the mirror with any inkling of honesty I have to own the fact that I am altering my appearance to increase the statistical possibility of having sex – there it is – the bare honesty of being a primitive being.

The element that fascinates me the most about fashions and the seeming care into how we look is really how primitive the entire endeavor seems to be. We put on war paint, camouflage for hunting, adornments for mating … all intensely dated and all directed at competition, survival, or procreation. I long for a time – perhaps it is in the deep future – that we will evolve beyond this very primitive stage of development and maybe start to exalt the things that are most important – **creativity and ideas**.

---

[28] Groucho Marx wrote "PLEASE ACCEPT MY RESIGNATION. I DON'T WANT TO BELONG TO ANY CLUB THAT WILL ACCEPT PEOPLE LIKE ME AS A MEMBER". This was sent in a telegram to the Friar's Club of Beverly Hills to which he belonged, as recounted in *Groucho and Me* (1959), p. 321.

NOTE 33 – BREAD AND CIRCUSES

In a world replete with "bread and circuses"[29], from the masturbatory daily use of Facebook to the inane twitter of Twitter, we are inundated with diversion after diversion. It is extremely difficult for most people to determine what are truly significant issues.

We are all searching for meaning or, perhaps more accurately, a feeling that we belong in the world. This generally requires others, their affirmation and approval. That has been somewhat of a problem in my own life, especially that lived as a scientist. My personal experience is that most people really don't want to know what you think or the actual facts – they often just want confirmation of what they already feel or "know".

An added complication is that the reality of reality is really statistical. Most answers are not simply YES / NO. Most complex things are YES / NO / MAYBE / INDETERMINATE. I am not trying to be obtuse in any way. The maybe stems from not having enough data to definitively determine whether something is indeed YES or NO. INDETERMINATE is a much more vexing thing. Indeterminacy most clearly comes up in mathematics and physics but, in general, it means that there is no method available that will yield a definitive answer.

Perhaps the most important and most poorly understood mathematical / philosophical determinations was delivered to us by Kurt Friedrich Gödel (an Austrian, later American, logician and mathematician). In 1931 he presented two incompleteness theorems. **Gödel's first incompleteness theorem** first appeared as "Theorem VI" in the 1931 paper *On Formally Undecidable Propositions of Principia Mathematica and Related Systems I*.

"The first incompleteness theorem states that no consistent system of axioms whose theorems can be listed by an effective procedure (i.e., an algorithm) is capable of proving all truths about the arithmetic of the natural numbers. For any such formal system, there will always be statements about the natural numbers that are true, but that are unprovable within the system. The second incompleteness theorem, an extension of the first, shows that the system cannot demonstrate its own consistency."[30]

---

[29] The Roman poet Juvenal (Decimus Iunius Iuvenalis - late 1st and early 2nd century BCE) was the author of the *Satires*. Perhaps more memorable was his coining of the phrase "bread and circuses" (in *Satires X*) that, in its simplest form, is a rather scathing commentary on the common man's preoccupation with the immediate and superficial. More to the point it seems to be a commentary on the general preference in governing to divert attention from truly serious and difficult matters.

[30] https://en.wikipedia.org/wiki/G%C3%B6del%27s_incompleteness_theorems. Retrieved 10/04/2016.

HOLY CRAP ON A CRACKER ... powerful axiomatic systems cannot contain all true statements about themselves! WOW! Let me see Kim Kardashian or Gwyneth Paltrow get their tiny little brains around that piece of incredible logic. This is the bread and we are left with the circuses.

If we do decide to pay attention to some of the greatest minds of all time instead of watch reality TV then perhaps we should consider the real importance of the development of statistical mechanics which grew up hand in hand with quantum mechanics and out basic understand of the atom. Most of us have been exposed to the Bohr atom in high school. Unfortunately, it has little to do with what Bohr actually thought or intended because it is usually presented as a negative electron orbiting about a positive nucleus. If anybody was awake in physics class just before the chemistry they would have remembered that "unlike charges attract" ... so why doesn't the electron just fall into the nucleus???? Well, that kept me arguing with a couple of teachers for days.

Instead of presenting the atom as it may well be they chose to simplify to the point of being totally incorrect. It would have been easier and much more informative to talk about the fundamental notion that Christiaan Huygens (1629-1695) had about light as a wave versus Isaac Newton (1643-1727) who held that light was like a particle. Perhaps light is neither wave nor particle. Perhaps an electron is both like the photoelectric effect that was explained by Einstein. The electron, at least within the atom, behaves like a wave. It is travelling at the speed of light and is effectively everywhere around the nucleus at basically the same time – it can't crash or fall. The point I would make here is that an electron has a statistical existence within different realms.

Chance dictates much more than we think and we usually don't stop to think about. What is the likelihood of winning the jackpot, let us say, the California Mega Millions Lottery? About 1 in 259,000,000. According to the National Weather Service the odds of being struck in a given year (estimated total deaths + injuries) are 1 in 1,042,000[31]. In other words, you are 250 times more likely to get hit by lightning than win the jackpot. Do people ever think about this for even a second before they buy their tickets? Probably not and, of course, we have sayings like "You've gotta be in it to win it!" However, the odds are much higher that lightning will get you.

So is this flagrant self-deception part of the "bread and circuses" phenomenon? Perhaps. Unless one is an ardent conspiracy theorist who believes that the government has allowed lotteries to keep the masses guessing and focusing on anything else but government then it is a conspiracy.

How much diversion do we really need? Do we have to always be on the cell phone? Do we really need to celebrate graduations from grade one? I am absolutely confident we could all do much better.

---

[31] http://www.lightningsafety.noaa.gov/odds.shtml. Retrieved 10/04/2016.

NOTE 34 – ART HISTORY CAN CHANGE LIVES

Just because I live near an existential black hole it does not mean that real events don't also happen in my life that bring me to an abrupt stop in my tracks ... like I totally missed something that most other people got.

As my life in the nuclear industry became more and more restrictive and much less exciting and I had lost a really decent boss to inherit the boss from hell, I increasingly drifted away from what most people would call a normal life. My wife was madly working her way through medical school and we had less and less to discuss partially because much of what she was loving was what I had long before learned to mistrust if not openly detest ... doctors. Don't get me wrong, there are great individuals in any field but the stunning mass of doctors are reasonably poorly educated and disproportionally arrogant and dismissive of the rest of us (basically everyone who is not an M.D.). So in typical, self-protective fashion, I decided to occupy the non-existent spare time I had by doing a part-time degree in art history.

There were many reasons for this turn of my thinking but one of the things that struck me the most was how different art history was from my own background and training as a chemist. A couple of years earlier I had been a student advisor to the only two women in senior level chemistry ... and they were both very attractive[32]. That did not change my mind in nixing their request to have art history as an elective in their final year. This brought instant protests and a surprisingly elegantly worded complaint to the department chairman about how "unreasonable" I was. This I took as a personal commendation. The chairman asked me if I was being a tad extreme and my only response was, "How long have you known me?". That was apparently the end of it until a few evenings later when I was having a beer with some of my students at the graduate bar. The two women asked if they could have "a word" – that never means what it says – it's always more than a word.

I got a second beer, changed tables, sat down with them, and prepared to be entertained until I lost it. They both opened with minor rankling about how unfair the system was; I assumed they meant undemocratic which, for me, signified a good thing in academic terms. "Unfair? Interesting. Explain!"

"Why do you get to have the final say on what we can actually take as courses for our degree?"

---

[32] There is nothing explicitly bigoted in this statement in that beautiful women can be smart but often don't feel the need or pressure to be perceived as such. Why get an advanced degree in the sciences to be able to buy the BMW for yourself when you can fuck for it at very much less cost and effort. A sad commentary but I'll own what I said! By-the-way, if I could fuck someone and get a BMW for it I am there in any desired position and call me slut!

"Oh, oh, oh, very poorly phrased question to which you should have already formulated a most simplistic answer ... because I can!"

This response brought a very welcome silence. I believe enough to savor not one but two good mouthfuls of beer. Instead of quelling the masses my response had the opposite effect. They both got a little irate and started in on me as if we were dating. Due to the instant and high-pitched cacophony the bartender came over to the table and asked, "Sir, would you like to have these women removed? They seem to be bothering you?" It was wonderful. Two years before I had been the bar supervisor for the graduate students' union and I had hired most of the existing staff. Fear is often more gratifying than understanding.

Both of the women were more than a little confused by the bartender's question and were probably really pissed-off at the answer. "It's OK they weren't bothering me as much as annoying everyone else."

BLESSED SILENCE for one minute minimum (a very long time in any mixed company). At this point I was supremely happy to be sipping my beer in silence with the complete security of being in my own protected environment.

More moderately the criticism continued with "What is your problem with art history?"

"Was that a question or admonition? If you wish to perform an *ad hominem* argument it is best to direct it at something that is specifically deficient in my character and behavior than some generic complaint that will never stand up to any serious scrutiny – by-the-way, art history is a fabulous fiction."

Again, a joyous silence brought more beer to my thirsting soul. Unfortunately, this pause was very short and one of them (I only remember that her hair was raven black and totally riveting) said "We think that you are biased and actually don't know very much about art history.

Bad move in debating strategy! "Would you care to test my knowledge of the history of art on a wager?" That was my macho response but the point was that if she wished to make any point at all with me that would not be the correct tack.

Her compatriot immediately stepped in with the correct approach (for me, at least) and she then laid down to gauntlet on the field of honor. "Will you let us take the course in Renaissance Art History once you have personally decided that it is worth doing?" Ballsy girl ... done.

I entered both the art history course and multivariate calculus as pending electives until I had made a final decision.

On cue, both of them showed up in my lab on the evening of the first lecture. I will never forget the circumstances – it was given by Dr. Warren Tressider, an Australian who had gleaned credibility by going to graduate school in England and thereby permanently modifying his provincial accent. The topic was Michelangelo and the designs and execution of the Sistine Chapel ceiling. The experience was transformative. His delivery was sure, calm and comprehensive **but of highest importance to me was that it was ballsy, individual, unverifiable, unfalsifiable ...everything science was not nor could be!** I was totally rapt in his utterly subjective analyses of the personality of Michelangelo and the circumstances that led to the creation of one of the more problematic pieces of art in the history of art. The hour passed and I wanted more ... everything, the entire story ... true or false didn't matter.

We left the lecture and I had absolutely nothing to say. They had won – I was a student of art history. In-and-of-itself this would qualify as a NOTE but it was far more encompassing for me. Warren Tressider encapsulated everything that I was not. He was in a discipline that did not require verification – opinion was enough – conviction was compelling – delivery was essential. I was completely envious. My world had always been about proof, replication and verification. His was a world of belief and conviction.

The women had proven their point but the outcome was much more complicated than they had ever anticipated. I would very soon go into the nuclear industry, get bored fairly quickly, regret my poor judgement (pretty much a constant component of my adult behavior), and enroll my-self in a "part-time" undergraduate degree in Art History at my *alma mater*, McMaster University. Why I have put quotation marks around the part-time is that it became a fanatic venture that was anything but part-time. Since I managed my own time at work I could do just about anything that I wanted so I simply went to every available class and spent my evenings and all other time doing the work I had committed to do for my pay check.

It was crazy but perhaps one of the most productive periods in my life. I avoided the inevitable discussions I did not wish to have with my wife about medicine. I did not have to avoid telling her what I was doing at work that was classified and that I couldn't tell her anyway. I could avoid supervising scientists who did not want to be supervised by someone younger and someone who clearly did not give a shit what they did. I could explore an entire field where I could actually express myself and not worry a bit about reputation or career – in fact, I might improve both if I just went ahead and said what I wanted to say. WOW ... GREAT!

This quasi-ideal state of affairs continued for about two years until I had accumulated enough credits to graduate. The journey was much more formative and interesting than I had ever imagined. On the way I had the pleasure of tangling with Professor George Wallace, a professor of art and art history, who was a very well-known and accomplished printmaker. I took a reading course (one-on-one) with him on the "Identification of Print Media" (my title). I will say in all honesty that it was the best course I had ever taken in my life and it was also one of the most demanding. After an initial meeting I provided him with a list of 19 books that I thought might be important for my "edification". His response was typical (as I was to learn very quickly) and he said, "There isn't much time you had better start reading". He meant that literally. I was naïve enough to think that he may suggest a few books but not all 19!

In addition to that he insisted that I actually produce at least three different prints (different media) to look at critically *post facto*. I learned more in a single course than in any other I had ever taken – probably by a factor of 2. My final "exam" or perhaps it would be better to call it an interview was in excess of 3 hours in his office. My first "test" was to suck the corner of 10 pieces of white paper and to determine what level and type of sizing had been used to prepare he paper. This was bizarre by most standards but when he explained the purpose of it to me it was totally appropriate and very clear. Papers are treated in various was to accept or reject printing materials and to stand up to handling and the environment in selective ways. Was it glue (what type), synthetic (what type), what level / amount (why? ... for what purpose), how did the treatment relate to paper type and projected printing medium?

The next part of the "test" was to go through a stack of 100 prints (all of which were his personal property) and determine all of the techniques used to produce the print, the possible country of origin and the approximate datation. I was in my personal heaven. It was if I had been designed to be in this place and in this time being tasked by this particular person. It seemed, for that short but incredibly intense time, that I had finally found my purpose and something that I was really good at and intensely interested in.

At the end of the period he asked me for my three prints. I presented them very hesitantly and with the very strict reminder that I was no artist. He quickly looked at two and deposited them on his desk and then held up the third, a linocut, that I had freehanded as a copy of and dullard's tribute to Picasso. Picasso had created a pregnant woman executed with a single line and incredibly sure hand. I had printed it in a very bluish-teal ink. He asked me if he could keep it and I immediately said yes. He then handed it to me and asked me to sign it. I was totally in shock but I reached out, signed it and gave it back. Without another word he reaching into his desk and handed me an etching of St. Peter clutching his head as a cockerel was pulling at his hair. He signed it, handed it to me and said that he had just finished a series and thought that it "particularly suited me". To this day, so many years later, I am unsure of his meaning but what I am incredibly sure of is the permanent positive mark it left on my soul. Is the piece valuable? I have no idea. Is it priceless? YES – to me.

I never asked my mark but when I got the transcript it was an A⁺. Several people asked me about the course because he was somewhat legendary and miserly with marks. When they asked what mark I got and I told them not a single person believed me. For the first time in my life it was OK that they thought I was lying – it was unimportant what they thought and, for me, completely personal – all between George and I. Oh George ... would that I could ever be half the teacher / mentor you were!

GEORGE BURTON WALLACE

Born: June 7, 1920, Sandycove, South County Dublin, Ireland
Died: July 17, 2009, Victoria, British Columbia, Canada
M.A., Philosophy, Trinity College, Dublin
Diploma in Fine Art, West of England College of Art, Bristol
Member, Royal Canadian Academy of Arts (RCA)

NOTE 35 – CLOUDS IN 17th CENTURY DUTCH LANDSCAPE

The initial introduction of art history into my life changed its course drastically. "Clouds in 17th Century Dutch Landscape" is really more about a relationship than about art history *per se*. It is a tale about Dr. Glenn Scott a profound personal influence for me both academically and personally as I strongly suspect he was for so many others.

Glenn died from ALS in Rome - a place he came to love. It took me two days to stop crying. I must say that the world was a much "smaller" place without Glenn in it. Almost no one knew that we were close and that was irrelevant. My own father never merited a tear and my mother got a sneer – much to my discredit. In fact, my eldest sister, was quite upset with me several years ago when we she insisted on discussing our long dead mother and I resorted to quoting a Canadian author, Robertson Davies[33], who said of his mother "Oh, these good, ignorant, confident women! How one grows to hate them!"

Glenn exuded love for art and beauty. He was profoundly and deviously intelligent. He would observe someone like a lioness observes the terrain and details when hunting. Then he would formulate the best way to get to them, inspire them, without frightening them away. He was outrageous, extreme and delightful. How he kept his job as an openly and unapologetically gay professor at a relatively conservative university (McMaster) was beyond me but that was all irrelevant. His specialty was 17th Century Dutch painting.

I loved his insights on compositional elements in landscapes and seascapes and I chose to do a major paper on "Clouds" for a seminar course. When I handed this in as my topic he said that we should "Perhaps discuss this a little". That is generally a bad thing to hear from a professor. As a buffer I offered him a drink at the graduate bar and he accepted immediately. After the usual trivial small-talk the real conversation started with a simple but incisive observation, "You don't sound like or think like an arts student".

I was sipping a double Cuba Libre at this point and I paused to pick the correct tone and response. "A+" was all that I said.

He smiled and then said very casually and with complete accuracy [absolute quote], "Disaffected scientist".

---

[33] Robertson Davies. *Fifth Business* (1970) "I Am Born Again", Section 4.

I waited a bit, trying to be sanguine, and replied, "Perhaps we should test your acumen and ask which type."

He drew back a bit and said "Chemist". Holy crap, I was stunned and then I thought that he could have easily looked up my academic background so I looked straight into his eyes and accused him of my suspicion. His response was simply, "No, it just seemed clear to me. Nothing wishy-washy, decisive and terse, evasive when necessary, creative and totally prepared to just make something up that sounds credible as you watch peoples' reactions." Again I was stunned but he was right and I realized that he was continually integrating the cognitive styles of the people around him.

Now I was really concerned that things could escape my control as I was trying to complete the degree as soon as possible.

"Clouds … well you chose an amazingly large topic for a seminar talk".

"Well, I did make the operational assessment that my intended title may not be too acceptable so I shortened it".

"So do I have to pry that out of you or do you just want me to buy the next round?"

"If you buy I think I can tell you that my title was going to be "The Meteorological Significance of Clouds in 17th Century Dutch Landscape: A Guide to Minor-Master Connoisseurship" – a bit verbose even for art history don't you think?"

His reaction was completely unexpected. He threw up his hands into the air and he said "Really? Really? Wow!"

His reaction resulted in a long night of animated discussion punctuated by far too many drinks.

The essential core of what I told him was, despite what I had been led to believe, that I did not see Dutch landscape painting as realist painting. The Dutch were clearly not *en plein air* painters but they did indeed study individual clouds very carefully. They were consummate at composition and used clouds like they would vases, skulls or candles to move the viewer's eye around the scene at will.

Unlike virtually all of the other professors of any discipline whom I knew he was openly expressive and excited and several times made me feel very uncomfortable by insisting that it was a brilliant insight. It was exceptionally clear that I would be doing exactly that topic with my title. I had never felt so clearly that I belonged somewhere or that the strange notions that often pop into my head might actually be of some interest or significance to someone else.

In the next class he asked me to "share" a five-minute "impromptu" presentation on problems in cloud painting in Dutch landscape. It was indeed impromptu and I said nothing but my stare directly at him should have spoken volumes. He simply carried on and told the class that he would present a series of landscape paintings and that I would dissect the composition from a meteorological perspective. When I started to say something to protest he then broke in and told the class that they were "in for a unique experience because I think that you will never get analysis on clouds from someone who has actually made them in a chamber in the Nevada". Crap, crap, crap, drunken tale telling can get you into trouble when you tell them to a person who has absolutely no inhibitions and does not respect the implicit boundaries of a private conversation.

The five minutes filled the entire 50-minute class. Every scene was deconstructed based on the clouds presented versus the actual meteorology under which one could see them in nature. The light direction in the landscape as well as surface and upper level winds were also introduced into the mix as seemed fitting. To be honest... I was in heaven, or in the heavens, or whatever... I was asked to do what I was designed to do – analyze, assess, deconstruct, report, extrapolate... science in the trenches, perhaps even science in the service of art.

Glenn stood up came over to me hugged me and said "That'll make a hell of a Ph.D. Thesis". I have no idea how my classmates felt but I was completely taken by surprise yet again by Glenn. All I needed was a mark for a fourth year art history course and he was already at the Ph.D. I already had a Ph.D. and that did not go so well for me. First of all, my mother never accepted that I was a doctor of anything – clearly the wrong kind of doctor. Secondly, here I was working full time in the Canadian nuclear industry and effectively a full time student in art history. Pathetic academic history and no future in a place where everything that I thought would be important was immediately going to be classified – no publications that I could be excited about only throw aways for my CV.

I am pretty sure that very few people knew I was married and many more thought that Glenn and I were a couple. He knew I was unhappy with my personal and professional choices and unrelentingly pushed me to do something for myself – something challenging and exciting. One evening Glenn realized that I was very upset. I had said absolutely nothing but he kept at me as to what was bothering me. I told him about a meeting I had at work where I was told that by the highest levels of management (a meeting and presentation in the President's office) that although the work and ideas I had for the handling of nuclear waste were "innovative" but that the corporation "could not sell the approach to the public". Perhaps the best work I had done ... unpublished and clearly DEAD. The director of research, who had championed my headstrong program, set up the high level meeting, and doubtless had manipulated other things, remained completely silent – no support whatever. Glenn listened intently and when I stopped talking he, as usual, knew there was more. Another drink arrived at the table and he said, "Dish!", so I told him that I had written my resignation and handed it in that afternoon. I had no plan, I had not spoken to my wife, it was a near six figure job in the mid 1980's and Glenn's only response was to hold up his glass and congratulate me. WOW. My wife, her parents, my boss, my colleagues would all have had diametrically opposite reactions to his. He was the only person in my life who seemed to really, genuinely want the best for me. It was quite overwhelming.

He asked if I would like to stay the night at his house.

"Glenn, you know I love you but I am sorry, I am very much heterosexual." (It was interesting that I did not say that I was married).

He smiled and put his arm around me and said, "I knew you would not be offended and I thought I would give it a try but I was confident you would refuse".

"So why did you ask?"

"Just in case you had a momentary lapse."

I smiled, hugged him very hard, and kissed him on the cheek. He was always very quick-witted and disarmingly charming.

I submitted my fourth year seminar paper that was in excess of 200 pages and I was just getting going on the major ideas and support for them. Glenn handed out the marked papers in the final class but all I got was a post-it note with "SEE ME". I really thought I had somehow crossed a line that I really didn't know existed. I went to his office (we had always met in some bar or other) and sat down. He handed me my paper with no mark. He then said something I will never forget; "I will give that paper an A$^+$ only if you promise to submit the topic as a Ph.D. thesis at Princeton – otherwise it is an F because it is too long and nobody in this department would ever admit to reading anything that technical." I asked if I could have a little time to think about it. He smiled and replied only, "Tick, Tock". Sounds a bit like Hannibal Lector but this preceded *Silence of the Lambs* (1991) by more than a few years – besides, Glenn was only "scary" in his passion for everything beautiful and interesting.

That entire interaction set off a major change in my life and thinking, I could actually escape and do a Ph.D. that I really wanted to do and actually publish something that people might read – that was compelling. I got my mark and decided to apply only to Princeton, with Glenn's very strong backing. In addition, I also applied to do a Master's degree in art conservation at Queen's University (the only program in Canada). I had the presence of mind to cover my butt and received a Canada Council grant to do the Ph.D. if I so wished. It was an intensely exciting but stressful time.

One of the major elements of stress was that I was going to call my wife on her promise that I could go back to school after she finished medical school. So I manned up and brought it up. She seemed to be tepidly OK with it but her parents (really her mother), in our forced biweekly bad cuisine dinners, had no problem telling me how selfish I was and that I was crazy to be leaving a high paying job to be a lowly student. I did expect a little support from my wife but got absolutely zero. I could only assume that she felt the same way as her mother but, for me, it was betrayal and I was going to do it - support or no support. There are simply times in one's life where there is nothing at all to decide – the course is obvious – regardless of obstacles or negative consequences.

Whatever was happening I was determined to go back to school – full time, for real. I was so much happier as a student than anything else and my recent run at doing an art history degree was irrefutable evidence. It is impossible to escape the irony that as I got older I became the student I should have been 10 or 15 years earlier. Another force that made the decision even easier was that fact that some of the best work I had ever done was never going to be published or followed up. All I can still say after many years is that burying medium and low level nuclear waste in a deep trench in Lake Superior is a far better idea than mine shafts in the Laurentian Shield (the intellectual scars remain).

I was clearing out my desk when the secretary to the director of research said that he really had to talk to me. In my mind there was little to discuss – what about I resign is unclear? A most bizarre event then occurred on my accretion disk. Instead of simply accepting it he offered me a sabbatical (a very unusual event for a corporation). I could lose all of the group I was supervising, do 10 hours a week on a "relevant" project of my choosing and get 1/3 of my salary. I had won the lottery! Nobody left to try to motivate, no more filler projects to clean up for people who had not got it right in the first place. JOY. I told him that I need some time to select a project. It turned out to be on Mossbauer spectroscopy with a side visit to the irradiation of paintings with slow neutrons. I figured I had complete secure access to very high neutron flux reactors and anyone at the station would never even bother to ask why I was irradiating paintings.

The saga of the clouds continued into a not-so-pleasant realization that leaving the protective cocoon of scientific research and academic protocol might not have been very wise. Having lit a match under the bridge at Princeton I went on to Queen's University for a very interesting two years in art conservation.

NOTE 36 – PARENTS, A PREGNANT NUN, AND ART HISTORY

While I was at Queen's University doing my degree in Art Conservation I was still working about 10 hours per week for Ontario Hydro. I would often just disappear from Kingston, drive 3 hours to Toronto, go to the lab, do work and periodically meet people for a drink since that's what most normal people seemed to do with their weekends rather than Mossbauer spectroscopy and slow neutron diffraction experiments on paintings.

I had recently become divorced and my new girlfriend went off for an internship in Los Angeles and I was left in a heightened state of arousal in Kingston to finish my second year. We had quite a torrid long-distance relationship with some chicanery on my part.

One weekend night Glenn Scott called me and wanted to meet me at a jazz bar in Toronto. As soon as he handed me my drink he started to grill me on how well I could read X-rays. I assured him that any smug medically trained radiologist was no match for me. Wow, yes, brash but I had been looking at x-ray crystal structures since I was a graduate student and I had been looking at X-rays and slow neutron scans of Zr-Ni reactor tubes for stress corrosion cracks. What he proposed was very outré (I think) and he invited me to go to Washington, D.C. with him to look at a problematic painting that was known to be by both Bellini and his student Titian. Glenn believed that there was at least one other "hand" (artist) in it Dosso Dossi.

I launched into my standard scientist disclaimer that I was not accustomed to dealing with analog images where guesses were involved. He laughed and put an arm around me and assured me that he would protect me from the "vicious art historians lurking around every corner". Little did he know how apocryphal a statement that would be!

So, there it was, Glenn and I in Washington, D.C at the National Gallery of Art. At the time, I was dating my second wife to be and she was in Los Angeles and I was still finishing my Master's degree in art conservation at Queen's University. However, she insisted that I stay at her parents' house in Chevy Chase. My first reaction to this was "How magnanimous" while my second, almost immediate reaction was "what an idiot I am". The positive side was that I could tell Glenn that I had no choice but to stay with my girlfriend's parents but the obvious negative for me was that I had to stay with my girlfriend's parents. I had already been married and just divorced. She was the eldest daughter in the family and the first likely to have the dreaded grandchildren. I was very aware that at least one of her siblings, Michael, hated me virtually as well as in reality, and I was very unsure of how her parents would take me.

The real reason that I was concerned was that the only contact that I had previously had with her family was typical of my experiences but clearly not of theirs. Her parents had travelled to Queen's University in Kingston Ontario to visit her at Halloween of the previous year and see the University before she left for Los Angeles for a year-long internship. I was dressed as a pregnant nun and they caught first sight of me as I was being raped by two drunken men named John (who were later to be two of our three best men). I don't remember exactly what transpired but I strongly believe that Susi made sure that she ignored the scene and drove her parents into a different local until I could collect my frazzled nerves and recoup my erstwhile virginity. It was probably an hour later when I officially met them but I find it hard to believe that people as bright as her parents could not run the odds that I was the only pregnant nun present at the party - they were simply polite enough to ignore it.

So – choice – stay with Glenn in a posh hotel in downtown D.C. or with my girlfriend's parents who had both previously worked for the CIA – anyone, including myself, should be able to see the inherent difficulties with both situations. I bravely and stupidly chose the parents. They were very kind (and hopefully forgetful) but the first dinner was clearly some kind of test. They had lived in Italy for some time and Bill had an impressive personal collection of Etruscan sculptural bits from digs. He showed me several things and then handed me a pair of clay testicles. I did know enough about archaeology to know that small simple sculptural pieces were often votive pieces, prayers and offerings to the gods for healing or other interventions. The only thought I had was not filtered and I said, "I hope he got his wish and got a much bigger pair". At least for Bill this was a sufficient passing grade for a boyfriend.

Glenn and I met at the National Gallery the next day and were escorted to the conservation laboratory by a curator whom Glenn clearly knew (probably ex-Princeton grad). Glenn was a real piece of work and when he got on a roll no one could stop him. He introduced me as an expert in neutron radiograph who worked with the Canadian nuclear industry (only half true or even a bit less) and he brought me along because he wanted to know how much data I could "tease" (my word) out of the existing radiographs.

I was given a large work table light box a big stack of x-rays. There were no notations and no apparent order so the first thing that I did was start to sort them out based on their position in the actual painting. The very first observation was that there was more than one set … yes set, not copy. The ones that initially looked like copies not only had very different exposures but slightly different positions in terms of how the x-ray was originally taken and overlapped.

After about an hour I finally sorted out two stacks based on position and relative exposure. There were absolutely no indications of when these were done and by whom and when I asked it seemed to cause an undue cascade of running about and whispered questions and directive from the adjoining room. Glenn returned and we sat down as I began to tell him about finding two sets and exactly why I found one superior because of its better judgement of the overall photo-density of the subject and exposure profile. I then pointed out the passages that I read as clearly original and pristine. They was the central figure group done by Bellini with no background or foreground present at all. He asked me why and I told him that they were the least photo dense, therefore the most thinly painted and there were virtually no pentimenti (corrective overpaints). Also, the figures preceded the landscape and I showed him this very clearly in a number of places. He was very pleased with this and went out to get another curator.

When they returned, I had already found distinct differences in the handling of different parts of the landscape. Again, Glenn was intensely interested but the curator was somehow stuck on how photo density might be an issue. I tried not to turn and dismiss him as I would have done any first-year physics student who was too stupid to get the point within 20 seconds (maybe 30 if they were hungover). I spoke more slowly than is my wont and reiterated what I had said to Glenn but with very conscious simplification. I had no idea whether that made any impression at all but continued on to state very clearly that if we had even a mediocre digitized matrix I could use the overlaps to create an isodensity profile, knit the images together, and then be able to do some pretty kickass determinations of who did what in very specific areas.

Well, that is where things began to get off the tracks really fast. First, the gallery had never recorded an absolute density / x-ray transmission standard. They had no digitized images and the museum had no on-site way to actually measure the optical densities. My verbal response was not contained or complementary, "You have got to be kidding!"

This was 1987 not 1787, the National Gallery in Washington, D.C. (ostensibly the finest art institution in the country), we were looking at a critically important painting in a transitional stylistic period in Italian art, within two hours of looking at god-knows-how-old unlabeled x-rays we were able to make fundamental new observations. I was totally unprepared for such an unreceptive reaction from the people in charge. Glenn did his usual charming best to herd the curator away and I took that as my cue to prepare to leave. Before I actually did pack up I paper-clipped the numeric designations to each x-ray and gave each a set number. I have the strong feeling that none of that survived past our visit.

Glenn and I went out for a drink and he was very excited about what we had found. He said absolutely nothing about the remark I had made and I found that incredibly odd. I brought it up and all he had to say was that, "I was entitled to my opinion and his only observation was that perhaps it might have been delivered in a slightly more diplomatic manner." So very much Glenn. He never brought it up again nor the fact that what we found was never acknowledged several years later when a quasi-major study of the painting was published by the gallery. I was completely appalled and he was completely sanguine – an incredible contrast of the two worlds we had developed in! For him it was normal – for me it was academically sleazy and totally unprofessional.

When I was asked by Susi's parents why I had not invited Glenn over to dinner I absolutely had to lie and say that he was incredibly busy. The truth was, I was already skating on thin ice with a family who thought I was marginal (recently divorced, raped pregnant nun) and bringing over an overtly gay, effusive, affectionate, and highly personally supportive Glenn was, most assuredly, a very bad idea.

NOTE 37 – DUANE, "YOU DIDN'T THINK IT THROUGH"

My first day at Queen's University Art Conservation Program was not as promising as I had hoped. I had already had somewhat of a parting of opinion with the director of the program who had wanted me to go into their "science stream" (only one position). Early in the selection process I told him that there was no way I would do that because I already had a Ph.D. in the sciences and "no affront meant, but it is highly unlikely that a formerly credible scientist who is an alcoholic and has to work at a smaller Canadian University has much to teach me that I don't already know." This really was not ego or arrogance, it was simply an analysis of the situation – something I had been trained to do and was very good at. Diplomacy and tact were clearly not part of my formal training. Anyone brought up in hard core science will support me on that. So, Ian Hodkinson accepted me in painting conservation but almost on day one … since I seem to have made my point that I shouldn't be made to do any of the "science courses" he, along with the resident scientist, decided that I had to make up for all of them with other Master's courses outside of conservation – SIGNIFICANT HURDLE.

As I made my way to my bicycle I met one of the other senior students (Susi) who, told me considerably later, that she thought I was a bit possessed when I started ranting to her that Ian hated me. At that first meeting she did volunteer that Ian hated everyone but I was not very much in a mood to be consoled. I got into two graduate courses in Art History. They were demanding but very satisfying and a distinct counterpoint to the physical side of art conservation.

Unfortunately, another difficulty arose or perhaps it is better to suggest that I brought it up. Ian had entered the art history courses as required not as elective. When I saw this change sent by the registrar's office I immediately did what the average student would likely never do – I went to the dean. We had a nice chat that centered around the official curriculum of the Art Conservation program and that fact that the science professor involved had pointedly asked me not to take his courses and personally waived the necessity for them. I then put him on the spot by asking whether the university routinely allowed Department heads to alter printed curricula on the fly and arbitrarily add required courses from other faculties. There was no hesitation or prevarication. He said very clearly and emphatically "Absolutely not!". It was the speed and emphasis of the answer that alerted me to the fact that this seemed to be an ongoing issue and I just happened to be in the way. The dean assured me that it would be dealt with immediately and said that, given my background, and the circumstances that I would not have to do any extra or external courses. At this point I said that I had no intention of dropping the art history classes but I would very much like his authorization to change them to qualifying courses for a parallel Master's degree in Art History. This brought an unexpected pause and a genuine smile as he said that it would be his pleasure. Wow – I obviously walked into a mini family feud or something!

A couple of days later Ian came into the lab where everyone worked all afternoon most days of the week and asked me to come to his office that was immediately across the hall. He proceeded to tell me that after long consideration he had convinced the dean to allow me to take the art history courses towards a separate Master's degree. Although it was unusual, it was due to the fact that the administration thought so highly of his student selections and management of the program that it posed no problem. Holy crap on a cracker ... and I mean crap. I had not seen that much shoveled in one spot by anyone. My only response was "Bullshit, bullshit, bullshit ..." as I walked out of his office back into the lab.

The utter silence in the lab, which was usually filled with good-natured chatter and banter, should have been a dead giveaway as to the decibel level of my interaction with Ian (at least the final 3 repeated words). He did not make his usual rounds of the lab that day and it took a couple of hours before people started to talk to each other. Had I assessed the situation properly it should not have been a surprise that no one spoke to me at all that day. I had the distinct impression that I instantly had acquired a terminal case of COOTIES – I was being shunned. I found out years later that my three words to Ian became a kind of meme before there were memes existed.

It was pretty clear after a year in the program and several interactions with Ian (none of those in my favor) that my former dog Jessie would get a higher recommendation for a conservation position in Canada than I would. He had placed almost everyone in the country and it was very clear that anyone who disagreed with him in any way better have a Plan B. Needless-to-say, I did not avoid heaping criticism on the raft of simpering sycophants with brown tongues who followed him around. Hey! It was the least I could do! Of course, I was not nominated as the Mr. Congeniality of Art Conservation.

My Plan B was very characteristically me – go somewhere else. In this case, I formulated a real plan. My new girlfriend was in LA, lonely and, crazily wanted me to come for her birthday in March. It was a nearly perfect setup. I insisted that she was being selfish and, given my unpopularity with certain persons in the department, I could not possibly leave my projects and studying for the finals, particularly in art history. I did plead with her to meet my friend John Nurse who was passing through LA on his way to a rifle competition. Initially she thought I was joking but I remained steadfast and earnest. She tried to entice me to come with the external carrot of a talk on clouds in Dutch landscape painting by the director of the Getty Museum, John Walsh, that was co-incidentally being given very close to her birthday. I refused and insisted that she treat John very well ... I described him vividly so she would not miss him at the airport.

In the meantime, I had phoned the Getty Conservation Institute and arranged an interview ... not so coincidentally for about the time of her birthday. After many evening conversations entreating me to come and trying to get me to admit that I was coming and not John, I phoned the evening before "John" was to arrive and I became very stern with her and said that John was important to me so she should be very nice to him and that she should not be encouraging me to jeopardize my future. She acted a little contrite and I reminded her of the flight and how to spot John.

I arrived at LAX and was very careful to slip behind the first pillar that I could see after clearing customs. She was waiting across a small open area and she had a small sign in her hand with John's name but she was NOT HOLDING IT UP high enough even for a 6'3" John to see. I watched her casing any potential person and finally someone came through that pretty much fit John's description. She looked crestfallen. I made my way around in behind her and watched the obvious signs of tension release when a very attractive woman ran up to the potential target and kissed him. At the point, I faked a deeper voice from behind her and said "Hey, big girl, what's up?" She did not turn to look but she clearly heard me. I then touched her elbow and she very quickly turned and was about to deliver a good slap. Instead, there were tears.

My visit to the Getty Conservation Institute was very enlightening. Apparently, the fact that I had a French last name, was not American (foreign), was the only Ph.D. scientist in the country (I believe in the world at the time) who also had a B.A. in Art History and soon would have a Master's of Art Conservation were significant reasons to hire me after two hours of discussion. They set about getting me a J-1 research visa and we agreed that I would start in a couple of months when the academic year was officially over. I went back to my girlfriend to be suitably rewarded and to break the news that she would have to find a way to tell her parents that we would be living together.

She did remind me of a little technical problem with my plan. Technically I was really supposed to do an internship and not get a real job as a scientist at the Getty Conservation Institute. My take (which was happily correct) was that Ian Hodkinson (the director of the Art Conservation Program) would completely overlook that minor academic detail since I would clearly no longer be a butt-pain to him and would not even be in the same country.

There I was, new job with very great potential, eager girlfriend and housemate, Getty minions getting my visa … how could it be better? Even the talk by John Walsh was not bad. Afterwards I went up and introduced myself and told him that I was newly hired and had a very strong interest in meteorology in landscape painting. I told him that I had written a considerable amount on cloud meteorology and he asked me to send it to him. Naively (as usual) I sent a rather extensive exposition (near 200 pages) to him when I went back to Canada. I never got a response and when I worked for the Getty I tried to make appointments with him twice but his secretary personally sent his apologies that he was far too busy and would get back to me. I won't even start to get into the academic shit hurling game and digress to calling names and pointless accusations of plagiarism, or at least protecting the claim of originality that one did not have. No, I would never stoop to calling a major personality in the museum world a worthless, spineless, dishonest scumbag … no, that is completely beneath me!

The title of this note is inspired by my crystalline mental image of my now 23-year-old daughter with her hands on her hips saying in a very much less than motherly way "Daddy, you didn't think it through …

did you?" (a reprimand I have often received). NO Rila, I clearly did not think it through even before you were born!

NOTE 38 – FENCING FOR A WIFE

My early years at university were not at all about academics but about proving myself physically. The first things that I did were to join the fencing club and the sailing club. These were definitive plusses for me since I was highly confident that I would always be the last one picked for any team involving a sport. I had sailed competitively for a couple of years with my own boat (a Fireball) and I loved an old Errol Flynn movie *Captain Blood*. Be aware that I was not completely stupid and knew enough about modern fencing that it had as much to do with *Captain Blood* as I had any claims on looking like Errol Flynn. It was the metaphor that was much more important than the objective reality.

For almost the entire first year in fencing I went three evenings a week and never missed. I nearly killed myself doing what every other person was asked to do and few of them seemed to have any problems. Lunge, jump, lunge, double-step lunge. The lunges were easy – one can usually fake them and call it falling with grace. Adding jumps and extra steps to a lunge were considerably more difficult with one leg that only cooperated at about 10-15%. As was described from the outset – the point in fencing is to move your body with the greatest possible efficiency but to keep the point of your blade absolutely steady, so that your opponent would get no advanced information of your imminent and potentially fatal attack. An objective observer would have seen instantly that I sucked at it.

The lessons and the club were in the hands of the University's fencing team coach Mr. Fred Wach, who was also the coach of the Canadian National Fencing Team. Fred Wach was ex Hungarian cavalry and he had a very heavy accent that required high levels of concentration to extract the meaning of most sentences.

To anyone who had observed, Fred was "the velvet fog" because he could move backwards faster than any fencer in Canada could move forwards. More to the point was that he moved backwards so easily that one would lose track or possibly fall asleep.

One evening as the Canadian National team arrived Fred came over to me and asked me to stay. I had no idea why but I was delighted to be able to see a real fencing team practice (not our usual club group or even the substantially better varsity team fencers). Fred then told me to stand against a wall and just parry. I did exactly what I was told until after just a couple of minutes he came over and explained that I would be parrying the people that he sent to attack me. After two straight hours of being hit at least 3 times per minute my entire upper body was screaming in pain. I did not even take a pee break.

At the end of the evening, having been introduced to no one, I slumped down on the wall, and tried not to fall asleep right on the spot. Fred drifted over and told me to come one hour early the next evening – that was all.

I showed up on time the next day after having spent at least 30 minutes in the Jacuzzi. I thought my left arm would fall off from extreme overuse. Fred was the only one there. He picked up a foil pointed at the same position on the wall I had the night before and waited for me to position myself. He said "*en garde*" and then hit me at least three times before I could even start to parry.

"Dvane parry!"

At that point, I gave him what I thought was a very fast sixte parry[34]. Out of nowhere came a lightning fast strike that removed the blade from my hand. Not a word was exchanged. I picked up my blade, stood against the wall and started to put together a whole string of pre-emptive parries that I was confident could stave off most attacks... BZZZZ... wrong! I was immediately hit twice right behind my parry, almost as if I had drawn an arrow for him.

He walked up to me grabbed my left wrist very firmly and then traced an almost imperceptible circle but with an incredibly firm touch. He then put his blade against the bell of mine and most effectively showed me the critical nature of the attack angle and the roll that very acute angular control at my wrist had on his point. He was graphically illustrating physics; a language that I completely understood. We spent the balance of the hour working on the other three major quadrants for parries, quarte (upper right for me, a left-hander), septime (lower left) and octave (lower right). In each quarter he took my hand and reduced all motion to nearly nothing.

So few words were spoken in an hour it was very simple to remember what he said; "Dvane the speed is in your mind!" That totally blew me away. Within a few minutes the varsity fencing team arrived and I started to pack up my gear. Fred waved at me and pointed to the wall. I went like a dutiful puppy and for another two hours I was the "hit dummy" for ten members of the varsity team (5 men and 5 women). No pee no break no words. The next day was similar but it was 1 hour before the club was to meet. This time he would attack but with feints ... trying to get me to overcommit to a parry. The first couple of times I was way too wide and took an immediate hit. Then I tightened it up incredibly with almost no motion. Bingo, one successful parry! I lowered my blade in triumph and he peppered me with at least three hits in fewer than two seconds. We continued for about 30 minutes and then he told me to go have a drink of water but add that it should take no more than 1 minute to drink said water.

We continued until the club members came and when I started to join their ranks I was again directed to my place on the wall. I then became the universal hit dummy. Everybody got a chance to attack me with very limited possibility of being hit themselves because I was constrained to stay on the wall. Day

---

[34] Sixte parry - A rapid but tight circular sweep of the outside quarter of your leading fencing hand. See parries online.

after day (now five days a week) I did just this. One consolation was that my left arm no longer felt that it was going to fall off. The negative side was that, in a very short time, my left forearm was noticeably larger than my right. All of my concentration had been on not being hit … parrying. The essential element missing was any real attack. In our rest times alone I discovered that Fred's day job was as a kinesiologist so it was no surprise that he had a solution to most of my "problems".

One of the evenings when the National team members were scheduled to arrive within the hour he told me to "parry – riposte"; basically, to parry and then immediately reposition my blade with a forward motion to establish "the right of attack". We did this for a few exchanges and he removed his masked and explained more slowly than usual – as if I were hearing or mentally impaired – "Dvane the point is to use the point". The problem was that I would extend my arm to attack but his parry was so fast that there was no way I could get in. I started to say something and all he said was "faster". We speeded up to as fast as I could possibly respond and still nothing.

He then took off his mask, laid it on the floor and again, as he so often did, grabbed my hand and shook it in very vigorous short stokes moving slightly forward. Without any words, he remasked and started his attacks again. I tried to do what I thought he had shown me and I still failed to get past his parries. The only positive thing I could say was that my own parry had improved immeasurably under his tutelage and the simple fact that I was probably the most habitually attacked fencer in North America (at least in my mind). Again, he stopped and pulled up his mask as he shook his head and said, "Veep, veep (or vip, vip)!" – clearly, I had no idea even though I nodded. My total lack of comprehension must have been astonishingly clear even though I still had my mask on. He then took his blade attacked, I parried and I received a stingingly fast hit behind what I thought was a perfect parry.

It almost immediately dawned on me that "Veep" was actually "Whip" … use the blade like a whip! We restarted and I began to use this new tool with incredible delight and perhaps a little too much vigor. If I timed my riposte to seamlessly follow my parry my flicked blade would simply bend around behind his parry and hit him anyway. It was fantastic! I refused to take a break and he just walked away so that I had no choice but to take a break before the others arrived.

When the National team arrived, Fred told one of them to hook me and themselves up to a machine. This got a quizzical look but was done without question. All he did was nod at me. On the very first attack – parry, riposte (whip), bzzzz (the machine goes off). The fencer who had attacked me looked around and saw a hit against him. He immediately went and checked the leads on the machine and then came back to attack again. Instant replay. He shook his head, ignored the machine, attacked again in another quarter and was hit again. This time he definitively felt my point because I had not tried it in that quarter while practicing with Fred. In the one hour with Fred I had to have made more than 100 hits so I had already had considerable practice. Two more hits went more-or-less the same way. Fred stood up with both hands in the air, one with a closed fist for my opponent and the other opened for me – 5 hits to 0, victory!

Over the next two hours this happened with six other members of the team (not all 5-0 scores but the most number of points scored on me was 2). As I packed my gear there was a very notable change in the general atmosphere. Fred said nothing as I walked away but I dare say that my normal limp was probably a bit more proudly apparent.

The next evening was the regular club and varsity team night. I showed up, as usual, one hour early and Fred hooked the two of us to the machine. I was now incredibly keen to show my new skills. Within the first ten exchanges he had hit me 5 times to my 0 on him. This was yet another time where I had no idea of what the problem was so he came up beside me and shoved my elbow into my hip and added a little slap to emphasize that it should stay there. He had stated so many times, both for me and other fencers that minimal movement was the key to speed. It was clear that I had been moving my elbow and the number of hits he just delivered were an unequivocal measure of how much I was moving it out of position and thereby nullifying my own defense. In the very short time that I had been allowed to attack it was clear that it was negatively effecting my defense. We exchanged three or four more times and he came up beside me held my elbow on my hip and made me parry – riposte 20 or 30 times – basically until I couldn't hold my blade any more.

After a few minutes rest we resumed and I managed to keep my elbow in and I finally scored a point before being hit. At that point, he partially removed his mask and shook his head, "Dvane, Dvane, Dvane, your elbow. Now we learn the Russian Way!" I had no idea what the "Russian Way" was but I knew it was going to be special.

We squared off and he made a series of complicated attacks as he very quickly moved in and out of range. As I reached forward with a whip to his sixte parry he raised his defending hand very high, cleared my blade completely out of the way and laid the nastiest flat-bladed whip on the tip of my elbow that was no more than three inches from my hip. It hurt like hell through a jacket and plastron. I could feel the welt rising before I could reach over to rub it with my right hand. AH – the Russian Way was clear – also indelibly etched in my mind. If there was a way to surgically attach my left elbow to my hip and still be able to fence I would have opted for the procedure immediately.

Just before the club people arrived Fred, with no words, handed me an ice pack and pointed back to my position on the wall. I stuffed it down my jacket and onto my elbow, enjoying the very tight fit and the rapid numbing.

I was loving my new position as the virtually impenetrable hit dummy that could now hit back! This provoked open anger in two of the varsity team fencers who just got wilder and wilder trying to get a hit as I peppered them with whips that they clearly could not even feel. All that is necessary to set off the machine on a properly set foil point is 500 grams (virtually nothing). Fred stepped in both times when things were getting out of control and sent them home. I felt very badly because I had no idea anyone would react that way. I had been hit so many times without being able to hit back - I really didn't get what their problem was.

Towards the end of the evening the men's team captain came over to me and gave me a set of maps and registration instructions for a tournament on the weekend. I thanked him for the invitation even before I looked at what he handed me and he very coldly said, "It's not an invitation, Mr. Wach expects everyone on the team to be on time and properly dressed."

WHOA! I tried to remain calm but I'm am confident that I stood slack-jawed for some time. I was on the team – holy crap, nobody ever chose me for a team in my life (well, not really true, there was chess). I had never even been to a tournament let alone been in one. I assumed I would be fencing foil because that what I did most of but in my duties as hit dummy I had also had to fence sabre and epee although very seldom.

I was very jazzed to be going to my first tournament but had absolutely no idea what the rules were even though I had tried to research things as much as possible, this was not very easy in 1975 given the raggedy state of the Internet. However, I did look up protocols and international rules so I had some idea. On the Saturday morning, I showed up early and looked at the line-ups. It seemed that Fred had decided (without telling me) I would be fencing all three weapons. As I had already learned, you didn't ask you just did what he intended or at least gave it your best shot.

It was incredibly fortunate that I had fenced so much in the prior year. The level of activity at the tournament was near zero compared to what I had done virtually every day. Also, I was used to being attacked by some very good fencers so I was completely unintimidated. My first foil bout was over in about 3 minutes (5-1). The second, third, and fourth were less than 2 minutes each. The last one was much longer and against a very good fencer. He recently had entered the University of Toronto but was from France. He was notably better than anyone on the National team and I lost to him 4-5. So, the day went and I only lost one bout after fencing five in each weapon. I really had not thought about anything else but fencing. For the day our team, McMaster, won all three team events. Fred had said nothing to me the entire time until the end of the day and then all he said was that I had to move more convincingly for the Frenchman.

As I was packing up my gear the team captain came over and this time very warmly shook my hand and thanked me. I was totally clueless. I only found out later in the week that that was the first win in any weapon for the team that year. Fred said nothing and I was then sure that, for him, it had nothing to do with winning – it had to do with the art of it.

We became very close and I would periodically ask him questions about his past since no one else seemed comfortable enough to do so. After a particularly demanding tournament we sat down and had a drink together. I asked him about Schlager dueling[35] that was very common practice in European Universities when he was a student. The duels were often very brutal and the scars were worn with strange and great pride. I asked him if he had been in any duels. He said that he had been in many. I must have immediately looked very skeptical as I asked, "Why don't you have any scars?"

His response was so appropriate, so Fred, "Dvane somebody has to win and somebody has to be smart!" Fred nurtured me and saw something in me that I had not seen in myself … the inability to quit. He knew I would do almost anything until I dropped. From him I learned to love the mechanics of a really primitive and simultaneously sophisticated endeavor. The other thing that Fred and fencing brought me was my first wife, Penny. From the first night, she showed up at the club Fred could see that I was completely captivated by a woman who could do perfect splits standing up against the wall. He asked me if I would "mind" tutoring her. As any good Canadian would reply (although I kept this only in my inner monologue) "Do bears make big potty in the woods? Damn right!" My verbal reply was simply that I would find some spare time. He smiled. He knew!

When I left McMaster, I left fencing forever – there was no Fred – there was nothing special about it without him. He had made me a very good fencer. I won many individual fencing awards but the only medals I kept were a Bronze for team foil for 1975 and a Gold for team foil in 1976. The only teams that would grudgingly have me and I did my very best for them.

---

[35] "Dueling scars (German: Schmisse) have been seen as a "badge of honour" since as early as 1825. Known variously as "Mensur scars", "the bragging scar", "smite", "Schmitte" or "Renommierschmiss", dueling scars were popular amongst upper-class Austrians and Germans involved in academic fencing at the start of the 20th century. Being a practice amongst university students, it was seen as a mark of their class and honour, due to the status of dueling societies at German and Austrian universities at the time, and is an early example of scarification in European society.[1] The practice of duelling and the associated scars was also present to some extent in the German military.[2]

American tourists visiting Germany in the late 19th century were shocked to see the students, generally with their Studentcorps, at major German universities such as Heidelberg, Bonn, or Jena with facial scars – some older, some more recent, and some still wrapped in bandages.[3]

The sport of academic fencing at the time was very different from modern fencing using specially developed swords. The so-called Mensurschläger (or simply Schläger), existed in two versions. The most common weapon is the Korbschläger with a basket-type guard. In some universities in the eastern part of Germany, the so-called Glockenschläger is in use which is equipped with a bell-shaped guard. The individual duels between students, known as Mensuren, were somewhat ritualised. In some cases, protective clothing was worn, including padding on the arm and an eye guard." https://en.wikipedia.org/wiki/Dueling_scar. Retrieved 07/31/2016.

NOTE 39 – A FLYING HORSE – "END OF THE TRAIL"

I have written very little about the art conservation work that I have done. I tried to understand why and the first reason I came up with was that many of my clients insisted on anonymity but on closer examination I realized that number had to be less than 10%. Another possible analysis would be that most of my work was uninteresting – that is categorically untrue. I was often very lucky and got to do some really cool things. Possibly the best explanation I can come up with for myself is that I continue to do work and I relish projects that challenge me but, in general, I would prefer not to place my work near the edge of the accretion disk. However, there are some pieces of my work that somehow mutated from conventional to a bit bizarre.

End of the Trail is the internationally famous slumping horse with its exhausted native American rider. It was executed by James Earl Fraser (1876-1953) who designed the Indian Head nickel and the doors for Annapolis. It is a plaster work about 8200 pounds, 21'10.5" high, and 17'5" long with a 21'1" spear (present parameters).

The history of the piece is remarkable. The sculpture won the gold medal at the Panama-Pacific International Exposition of 1915 (the world's fair held in San Francisco, February 20 - December 4, 1915). The primary purpose of the Exposition was to celebrate the completion of the Panama Canal. It was commonplace that sculptures so well received were cast in bronze and installed appropriately. However, WWI was already underway and all bronze was commandeered for casting into cannons. This is the likely reason that the plaster sculpture was cut into pieces for disposal.

Interests from Tulare County and the town of Visalia, California pooled together to purchase, transport and install the work in Mooney Grove Park. It is likely that there was direct intervention by Hugh Mooney himself. (http://www.visitvisalia.org/member/mooney-grove-park/515716/). In 1968, the plaster was moved to the National Cowboy Hall of Fame and was resorted. Visalia received a full-sized bronze (cast in Italy) in its place.

At the time of our work (1994-95) the sculpture was in the National Cowboy Hall of Fame (Oklahoma City, OK) and the museum director was Byron Price. They were in the middle of a capital expansion campaign and wanted the sculpture to become the centerpiece of the revitalized museum. He had been told by at least one exterior source that the plaster could not be moved in one piece and he then proceeded to request bids from several potential suppliers for moving and conservation services. Of all of those who responded, ConservArt Associates, Inc. were apparently[36] the only company who proposed to move the sculpture in one piece and were confident that the sculpture did not have to be partitioned.

---

[36] As reported to Duane Chartier in a private conversation with Byron Price. ConservArt was run be my ex-wife and me and still exists and runs very well, likely better, without me.

The sculpture had many cracks and could be moved several inches laterally with a few pounds of force exerted laterally (left to right side only) in any zone at or above the head of the horse.

The greatest challenge was to keep the piece intact rather than to break it into pieces as had previously been done. The fragility of the overall structure required some dynamic and possibly even novel engineering choices. A steel cage that was attached to the I-beam support base structure (clearly from the earlier restoration campaign at the hall) and fabricated around the sculpture. Chain links were welded on at various points to be able to run straps to secure the piece.

Despite severe ambient cross-chatter and both implicit and explicit criticism the loose tethering of the sculpture within the lifting frame continued. When individuals opine that "I wouldn't do it that way" the likely translation is "you are doing it wrong". It is a personal observation that everyone I have ever heard say such things has never been asked to or done anything particularly challenging or significant. Such comments are simply inane and annoying – not constructive. So, my responses are usually delivered in kind, such as "Nobody asked you how you would do it, did they?" The design intention was to allow flexure in the steel armatures of the legs while containing the amplitude of the overall movement of the upper structure.

The most tense operation was the initial lift of the sculpture and cage with a fork lift in order to place it outside the building to be "picked" by the crane. The 65-ton capacity crane was rigged by me (the crane company, appropriately, refused to take responsibility for rigging my structure) after I signed a release for the operator. The need for such a large crane was the long pick angle and need to lift over existing trees. The sculpture was swung across trees and toward the target transfer point which was a semi-trailer flatbed abutted to and leveled with the new foundation of the museum entrance. All of the move took place in front of the public and an array of cameras from local TV stations.

While walking the work across the muddy construction site I turned to a person who was dangerously close and swore at them as everyone had been told to stay completely clear. It turned out that the admonition was given to the museum director, Byron Price, who said (to the best of my recollection), "Don't worry Duane if it falls it is best that we both be under it." He was correct. My admittedly tiny reputation would have been completely ruined at that point (had I survived).

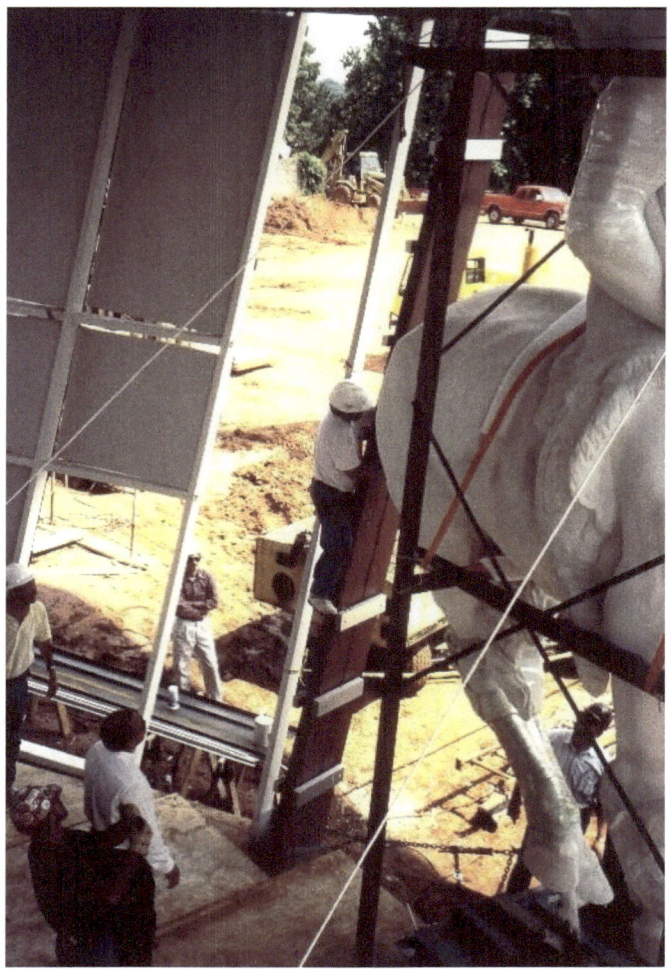

The fork lift was subsequently lifted onto the rear of the flatbed and the sculpture was guided through the steel framework of the new structure (with only 2" of clearance) and lifted onto its new base. The image shows me perched in a very unfortunate juxtaposition to the horse's ass. A commentary that has not escaped me many times over the years.

The sculpture was covered in plastic until construction was complete. It was then (almost a year later) that final conservation was completed.

The actual run time of the project was about 3-4 weeks but it was completed over one year due to the fact that the new building was being constructed around the positioned piece. The refabricated base, new spear and coating were only added after building construction was virtually complete.

The surface finish was a major conservation issue. It had previously been painted many times[37] and the paint layers were differential in color and peeling. The selection of a new coating was critical to the long-term stability and maintenance of the work. The new location of the sculpture was the centerpiece of the new main entrance with significant fenestration. Although the director of the museum and the architectural firm were alerted to the need for maximal UV and IR protection there was a clear decision to disregard significant conservation concerns. As is usual, cost was cited as a factor. In response, I floated an unusual solution, Keim[38] mineral coating was considered. Because the manufacturer was unwilling to provide a custom coating on short notice I created one by using ethyl polysilicate (SILBOND® 40) and raw white pigment (TiO_2). The simplified physico-chemistry of the system is that the polysilicate liquid undergoes hydrolysis over a period of weeks with atmospheric exposure and off-gases ethanol (normal alcohol) leaving a loose (non-film forming) silicate coating ($[- O - Si - O -]_n$) with incorporated white pigment.

The museum personnel were alerted to the fact that the coating would initially be very glossy but that would change over several weeks to be a matte finish. It was chosen because it is a non-film forming inorganic substance that has no reaction to UV light.

The spear is a 6061-T6 aluminum pipe with a carbon-fiber epoxy wrap and a thin plaster veneer. Its' very light and rigid construction allowed for a much more long-term and stable repair. The spear head was modelled after Fraser maquettes and smaller scale related sculptures. I am perversely proud that I properly armed a native American for the 21st century.

It is somewhat of a miracle that it has survived, even in its altered state, to this date. It is also rather bizarre that Visalia would have the only full-sized bronze. The positive read on this is that the maintenance of the plaster is job security for conservators into the deep future.

---

[37] There were many coats of paint that were applied during the period that the sculpture was displayed in Mooney Grove Park in Visalia. The total number and color range were not properly documented in the 1960's restoration and bronze sculpture preparation campaign. There were subsequent applications of white at the National Cowboy hall of Fame. Type of paint and time of application were not recorded.

[38] "Unusual" in terms of North American museum conservation. The coating of interest was a silicate "paint" developed for European architectural conservation – Keim mineral coating. Unfortunately, the color and consistency required were not available and the company indicated that it would takes months to produce.

What actually brought this project to mind is that in May of 2015 I got a call from the events director of the museum asking me to give a talk on the conservation work. This came as a bit of a shock since it had been 20 years since we did the work. I offered to give a talk on something more interesting to me and more topical but there was zero interest. So, I accepted the honorarium and the free trip before I integrated that I had no electronic media from that period, only slides and prints. I scrambled to get that together and it took me about a month to assemble the materials and rethink what had occurred so many years before.

I must say something that I often have to say … I was a complete bonehead in not realizing that 2015 was the hundredth anniversary of the Panama Pacific Exposition where the plaster was first shown. It took me a month to realize why the museum might want a talk.

It was very eerie going to the museum because when I arrived in the evening it was closed to the public but I wanted to make sure that everything was set up as requested for the talk in the morning. This included a lift for me to go up and handle the sculpture at the end of the talk and answer and questions.

As the coordinator and I walked towards the events center she called to me to follow her down the opposite hall and I had no idea why but I dutifully followed, but I think it was because she hadn't handed me the check yet. I was greeted by a special exposition featuring the actual moving of the sculpture with me moving on two large screen televisions. It was most unnerving to see a younger but much less fit me, madly directing many more people than I remembered. I was totally unprepared and told her that it creeped me out and I immediately walked away. I had never seen any of the footage and had obviously not been interested enough at the time to pursue it. Perhaps, as an art conservator I should have been but, at the time I was so focused on my particular responsibility (the sculpture and its safe handling) that I totally disregarded that level of external documentation.

Later I assured her that my reaction was just that component of my personality that often clicks in … I don't really want to be a member of a club that would have me as a member. She looked at me very strangely but that was that.

For people with a particular and strange disposition the Power Point presentation of the talk is downloadable on-line at (P.S. It is large … be patient):
http://www.authentica.org/End%20of%20the%20Trail%20OKC%20150914.pptx.

NOTE 40 – PEOPLE WHO I WOULD LOVE TO BE MORE LIKE – WILSON HURLEY

There are very few positive male role models in my life but I can lay legitimate claim to having one of the best. I met Wilson Hurley during a telephone conversation in 1990. I had been referred to him by Zora Pinney, who owned an art store in Los Angeles and who was very active in the art and art conservation community. It is critical to provide a little background here because there was much more to my initial reaction to his call than one might imagine.

I had just moved to Los Angeles with my new (but second wife) and we had the temerity to open a private art conservation business. Although we had been in Italy for two years we had both previously worked in Los Angeles. Susanne had worked at the Los Angeles County Museum of Art and I had spent a brief time at the Getty Conservation Institute when it was new and in an industrial / commercial complex in Marina del Rey. A very important point in any niche business and especially one in which "reputation" and perceived standing is important is being very careful to be associated "with the right people and be working on the right things".

Wilson's call came as a surprise but mostly for the incorrect reason – my unreasonable bias against things "western" like oater movies. Wilson had a slow mild southern drawl that made me want to extract the words from him at a much higher rate than they were being produced. In reaction, I spoke even faster than normal to fill in the space. He told me that he was doing a large landscape commission for the National Cowboy Hall of Fame. That information alone was enough to prompt me to find a way out. The key word he used was landscape and I quickly volunteered that my favorite landscape painter was Meindert Hobbema (1638 –1709) who was long dead. I was very obnoxious but Wilson totally took it in stride and suggested that we had come a little bit further than the Dutch of the 17th century.

He then told me that he had experienced some problems with a conservator he had hired and that he would like me to "come on board". I knew the person he was referring to but said nothing. However, I did understand why he might be having a problem. I told him the blatant lie that I was very busy and offered to find him some more local help and that it would take a day or two to get back to him.

The next morning, I got another call from Wilson and before I could protest about him bugging me too soon about a recommendation he broke in with "Duuuanne, I have spoken to a few people about you and they say you are sometimes a little brash and perhaps too quick to make judgements. I would like to propose that you take a little time to consider my request. I have arranged for a ticket in your name to Albuquerque on Southwest Airlines and, if you really can't help me after seeing my work and speaking face-to-face I would be willing to call it a draw." WHOA! I was really in some kind of western movie and I was more-or-less being challenged to a gunfight at noon! Of course, I said yes and arranged to go the next day.

That decision literally changed my life. I went to visit Wilson and Roz Hurley in their home high up above Albuquerque in the Sandia Peaks. Wilson was immediately welcoming and undeniably charming. He showed me his work and the progress he was making on a series of five triptychs what were to be installed at the Cowboy Hall of Fame in Oklahoma City. That location and name did not stick so much in my craw as the first time that I had heard it. I was concentrating more on a solution that Wilson might appreciate. I told him that we could do a number of things that had never been done on this scale before but I would like a few days to make a proposal.

He was one of my first large-scale projects and, without hesitation, was my best client ever! There are just so many reasons I can say this in the wisdom of hindsight but even at the beginning I could not asked for a better informed client. I told him on more than one occasion that he really didn't need my services. He started adult life as an aeronautical engineer and an air force pilot, he later became a lawyer, then a banker, and finally at forty years old, a painter. He loved history, cosmology, space, nature, physics, chemistry, engineering, gadgets, art and romance.

Wilson hired me to do what I do best … think, design, create. Even when I royally screwed up at the beginning of installing his paintings and I called him and said that it was all my fault and I would swallow the loss he said, "Duane we are in this together, I have every confidence that you will sort it out". No recriminations, no admonitions, no losses, only an unerring focus on the final goal. The money from the work allowed me to have children with some confidence that I could afford to feed them and maybe even educate them!

One day at a very mediocre lunch at the National Cowboy Hall of Fame cafeteria Wilson and I were discussing something quite outré and Wilson said several very interesting things about space-time. At that point, I turned to him and told him that regardless of his "style and guile, you cannot convince me that you are not fundamentally an academic." He then proceeded with both "style and guile" to deny it.

I immediately responded that I felt like I was being buried in a load of "bovine fecal matter" (exact quote). He just smiled. It was possibly the only time in Wilson's adult life that anyone responded in that way to his considerable charm. That ended our brief lunch save for the very telling hand on my shoulder as we ambled down the hall, back towards the installation.

Wilson Hurley, a towering man - nothing to do with being 6'4" - an imposing and adorable example of what the strange forces of nature can produce when it finally gets something right. Anyone who wishes to know what "being bigger than life is" should take a look at him on video and to experience some of his work. Useful information is available on-line in his catalogue raisonné (www.wilson-hurley.com).

My blundering on about Wilson cannot begin to say what I feel – I miss him and think of him often. Mahatma Gandhi said, "You must be the change you wish to see in the world." If, every day, I could be just a little more like Wilson I would be so much closer to being that agent of change. The real irony is that he was one of the very few people who I felt could accept me exactly as I am or, as he would say, "warts and all".

NOTE 41 – THINGS WE WISH WE HAD SAID OR NOT

I think that all people have favorite sayings or aphorisms. Some of us have them closer to the surface and some of us wish that they had even been closer to the surface so we could have used them as a formidable weapon in an argument, in self-defense, or simply in a vain attempt to amuse others and impress them with our erudition or, at least, our ability to steal the work and thoughts of others. This is pretty extreme because I have always believed that well-chosen quotations are often symbols of the highest respect.

The problem is that we so rarely are quick enough or prepared enough in our normal interactions with people to use a quotation wisely and incisively. Sometimes we manage say impressive and amusing things but not necessarily to those we were actually speaking to.

Although there are famous movie adlibs they really don't fit into what I am trying to capture here because they really cheat in that the originators have already thought about them within the context of a character or in reaction to already written dialogue. Perhaps my favorite line was from the replicant Roy Batty (Rutger Hauer) in *Blade Runner* who said:

> "I've seen things you people wouldn't believe. Attack ships on fire off the shoulder of Orion. I watched C-beams glitter in the dark near the Tannhäuser Gate. All those moments will be lost in time, like tears...in...rain. Time to die."

Although marvelous, not completely spontaneous.

A much better example of the spontaneous is a quotation attributed to the drunken Winston Churchill as said to Lady Astor.

> "'My dear you are ugly, but tomorrow I shall be sober and you will still be ugly".

Not nice in any way but imminently quotable and the mark of an exceptional wit.

One of my ex-wives has a very sharp tongue but it is never quite on time and the barb is then completely wasted. I do remember something that perhaps I should not have said when were initially dating because she never let me forget it. We were at a performance of a small but excellent modern dance company - Compagnie de danse Eddy Toussaint - dominated by very strong male dancers. However, there was one incredible female dancer named Anik Bissonnette. Immediately after the very prolonged applause died down she asked me what I thought and what immediately came to my mouth (perhaps not going directly through my brain) was:

"I would crawl a mile over broken glass to lick a bead of sweat off of her navel". In addition, I apparently leaned over and licked her cheek. It clearly wasn't all negative at the time because the poor mis-guided girl did marry me.

There are so many things in life that we should have said or should not have said. The trouble with the things that you shouldn't have said is that you can't go out and collect the sound waves and bottle them back up. Now, if one could do that ... the ULTRA Nobel Prize.

There must be a very large number of males who have been trapped either by their quick wit or, more likely, by their inability to parse the question actually being asked such as "Honey does this dress make me look fat?" Every male who bothers to pause for a second will be able to come up with the correct answer ... "Of course not dear!" It is an error to add any qualifications at all to such a question such as color choice, cut or anything else. It is totally hazardous to venture into the realm of immediate reaction or simple honesty. Examples of some very bad responses have often flashed through my mind:

"No, it's not the dress."

"The lighting is bad in here why don't you go into another room." [you are bothering me]

"Perhaps it is just muscle tone."

"No, I think that would be the adipose tissue." (Clearly the worst and something I might say but never have.)

Over many years of navigating the perilous relationship seas I cannot claim to possess any useful information that I could pass on about communicating with the opposite sex. Well maybe ... don't ever say anything to a non yes/no question without counting to 3 ... slowly. That may be enough time to process the question and to attempt some determination of its' real intent. That is really the best I can come up with, in my 64 years trying to figure out male / female differences. YES, THERE ARE INTRINSIC DIFFERENCES.

Oops, probably another *faux pas* in a politically correct but insanely incorrect world. If men and women were not created quite differently there would be many fewer children and my personal desires to go on an unrestricted boink-fest would be highly reduced. Whether one believes in religion and a divine creator or evolutionary changes (my preference) it is very clear that there are males and females of most species because they are supposed to boink, ostensibly to procreate. In the haste to boink I can certainly aver that I rarely, if ever, considered procreation as the goal. That may be an intrinsic biological irony or necessity in that I have not been given the full capacity to project the consequences of my actions when I am aroused.

NOTE 42 – THE GYM – A MICROCOSM OF LIFE AND DRAMA

I started this series of notes or stories with a foreword that featured characters from my new life that centers around the YMCA gym(s). It would be silly of me to omit some of the most interesting people whom I know.

Mallory ... Asian / Chinese / Filipino / Hawaiian (hell of an orgy, wasn't it?)/ pitbull, actress, personal trainer, sweetheart. Whenever I think of the Y she is the first image that pops into my mind. She's funny and feisty and dedicated to making sure that people do the very best they can. Sometimes this requires telling people to shut-up and really do some exercise – of course I am only reporting this second hand and have never felt the stingingly clear truth rip through my mandibular flexors. In large part, it is due to Mallory that I keep challenging myself, especially when it is so much easier to give in and just go get a glass of wine. That is not to say that I don't do that later but more as a reward than as a method of avoidance.

AJ ... academic engineer / economist with a strong sense of the ironic along with an admix of questionable Indian philosophy. I must credit AJ with many of my daily existential crises brought on by questions that he poses such as "how much exercise does one really need?" I personally feel that these kinds of questions should be black-listed in a gym. He has often caused me to go away and started me on the slippery slope of considering replacing all my physical workouts with virtual ones. This is a very attractive idea when one is tired and fed up of looking in the mirror for any signs of improvement. I suggested that we market a virtual exercise regime together and he rejected my pearl of wisdom. That left me brutally rebuffed but fundamentally unscathed.

Mike ... aka Squeaky Mike, swimmer, former printer, generous fisherman. He spends a great deal of time in the pool but most of it is in teaching others like Pena ("the Queen") how to turn and do other things. He is squeaky because the cheap thongs that he wears after swimming announce his arrival long before he actually appears. He is retired and much like the elder James, he tends to gather flotillas of women with whom he gabs in the pool.

Pena ("the Queen") ... larger than life Mexican woman who is Victor's wife and whom I have only heard him call "the Queen" or occasionally "my wife". She regularly stands up in her lane in the pool and bids a loud good morning to most who walk by. She often tells me I am late if she does not spot my truck parked on the street as they arrive.

On a recent morning, she got out of the pool as I made my way back to the locker room for something before I went to a class. She asked me to hug her but seemed a little surprised when I reached out my arms and did. She then said, "But now you are wet!" I threw up my hands to indicate that it was just water. Besides, I now had two impressively large wet breast imprints on my pristine white t-shirt. I am willing to bet that most men would wish their mornings would go this well. Or poor Victor ... he so has his hands full!

Vincent ... too young (29), too tall (>6'3" is excessive ... 5'2" is acceptable), too good looking (vexing), too nice (puke-some). Vincent is very affable but seems to have been trapped into making a living as a psychologist rather than a professional athlete. I officially met him one morning in the locker room as I was having an exhaustive or exhausting discussion with AJ about my hypothesis that one should name their muscles and regularly talk to them. My essential point was that we generally treat our muscles like crap and take them for granted and that if we gave them names and a little respect they might work better with and for us. Vincent was rapt in my teasing of AJ because my real sub-point was that much of Indian philosophy was Maharishi doo-doo. I then turned to him and introduced Timmy (my right triceps) and Tommy (my left triceps) who had just had a hell of a workout in a Group Power class.

Vincent's reaction was probably one of trying to determine what syndrome I had but I could not resist so I continued introducing other muscles to him like Quigley (my left quadriceps – a massive and well developed type) and Quandary (my right – "lazy retarded quad"). He told me that it was not generally advisable to use the word "retarded" and I had already formulated an anticipatory response. I asked him: "Do you mean to suggest that my slower, less strong, idle, useless, right quad would perhaps prefer to be typified as neuro-muscularly challenged?" I think that ended the particular morning's exchange. In my own defense, I can say that talking to your muscles is not so bad – you are never alone when you are schizophrenic.

In a recent "Core Strength" challenge at the YMCA Vincent was killing himself as someone officially counted his crunches ... 192 legitimate ones and then he got a second chance (illegal) to make it to 200. I was just a bit miffed. I lay down on the mat and started my own set. He went off to get some water and loosen up and when he returned I was at over 300. He stood and watched as I began to get more and more labored and slower and slower. I told the person counting to tell me when I got to 400. When I got the nod I petulantly added 5 more just to make sure that NO ONE could mistake the clear doubling. Vincent just shook his head in disbelief. From my prone position, I didn't bother to get up because I could give him my response right from where I was:

> "Don't you dare shake your head at me, you are half my age, twice my height, twice as good looking ... you deserve a good bitch-slap!"

He just laughed but there was likely some jealous truth in my commentary.

Roya ... killer abs! I had no idea who Roya was until the YMCA management decided that we needed a fitness challenge [like waking up in the morning and dragging one's sorry ass into the gym was just not sufficient!]. The second week of challenges was CRUNCHES. I had put young Vincent in his place the day before but when we passed the board with the results I saw ROYA ... 600. Six hundred, hell no, six hundred! My only thought was who is this superman. I went into the exercise room and asked Mallory who the hell the superman Roya was. She very quickly brought her finger to her lips and said, "She is right there". God what a dickhead I was... it wasn't Superman – it was Superwoman!

As Mallory went in the opposite direction I went to the triceps machine that she was working on and with no introduction I asked her if she was Roya. She nodded, I asked her to stand up for one second and then I just reached out with my left hand and grabbed her abs. YES! I know, totally creepy and no thinking preceded the action but there was no malice – I just had to feel them. They were like Kevlar. I swear that you could use her abs as body armor in a gun-fight. I was in complete awe and said as much as I shook my head and walked away knowing that I was toast – she was as fit as I will never be! Also, thank god, she has a sense of humor to go with the abs.

James ... (74) ex-alcoholic for over 27 years, serial pool socializer, smart, affable, scarred by the world and all the better person for it. He is often surrounded by women in the pool and comes into the locker room complaining that he is cold because he spent too long in the pool. I not so delicately pointed out to him that it was an occupational hazard if that is where you were attempting to get lucky! I also volunteered the pearl of wisdom that is a bit of a paradox that you actually get cold when you are trying to get hot.

James ... Greco/American economist, swimmer who helped me focus on what notes I would write and use (see foreword). I was carping one morning about how just about everyone in the gym was named James and although it was no tribute to their parents' imaginations it was a lot easier for me (more brain cells to devote to wine rather than remember more names). He then broke in with one of his amusing "My Big Fat Greek ..." family stories about how every second generation used the previous generation's names. That all went well until I started enquiring as to whether Achilles, Agamemnon, Acacius, Aeschylus, Aesop and a few others failed to have families so their names never were passed on. There was no real credible response. I did end the conversation by asking a question that he never answered on the pretext of being in a hurry to get to work. That was: "Where do you think those guys whose names aren't popular now originally got their names?"

Tatiana ... thin, far too fit, Russian mathematician at USC who lifts more weights than is normally considered tasteful. She brings in her Ph.D. students to exercise because she firmly believes in the adage "strong body ... strong mind". There is a flaw in this thinking however because she can out-lift the largest male that she has had in tow and I am positive I could hear his scrotum crinkling up after just one 55-minute class – I have not seen him since.

Chrissy ... Group Power instructor, gorgeous tiny Asian power lifter with a smile that makes me want to slap her.

Week three of the Core Fitness challenge – Single Arm Planks – I am in the lead all week – the first time that I am not trailing the unknown superman Sufiyan. Holy crap on a cracker... how pathetic my life must be when I have trained hard for a year and a quarter and my crowning achievement is that I am leading in a "contest" that shows that I am the best at emulating a board! OMG there are no real words for this other than something my daughter often says to me ... "Dad, you didn't really think that through; did you?" Well, I "won" and now a can say with confidence that I am the best plank that was stupid enough to join a contest that was half about planking and that sane people would probably steer clear of.

To add to the pathetic nature of this non-triumphant triumph I decided to celebrate "the win" with Chrissy on a Wednesday morning at 6:30 am at the gym by toasting her superior leadership abilities with some old vine zin. I needed the wine to get through her hour-long Group Power class where she definitively makes me look like crap as she smiles and does curls that remotely hurt my biceps from across the room. She is the sweetest, truly genuine person but I still want to slap her when she is smiling and the rest of us are dying.

Yoga instructor (name Orchid) ... personally responsible for me never wishing to take a second yoga class ever again! Although I had never taken a yoga class I knew many of the names of poses and had been exposed to the words of praise given by loyal acolytes. Many of the poses do look as their names suggest "cat, downward facing dog, tree" but others make no sense at all like "half hero stretch, sage pose, wind relieving". Well maybe wind relieving would be credible if you urgently needed to lay with your back on the floor and pull one knee to your chest in order to release a fart.

We did something called a "twisted eagle". She demonstrated and I must say that although I think of myself as a very imaginative person I could not, for the life of me, interpret the convoluted arms and legs as an eagle – not even one in the paroxysms of a final DDT induced neurological system breakdown. I could do the pose but it was very strange and I had no idea how it would be useful in any way in my world.

During the warm down and meditative section of the class she started with a quotation from Gwyneth Paltrow. Anyone who quotes Paltrow is certifiably insane! The only way Paltrow can say anything remotely sensible or comprehensible is if someone gives her a script (try to listen to an interview with her and you will immediately agree).

We were supposed to lie of the floor and reach out into the universe. She talked about how calming the universe was. Clearly, she had learnt nothing about astronomy or cosmology. To start there was the BIG BANG (not very calming) and then there are regular annihilations of systems with Class I and Class II supernovae. Of course, there are black holes that suck all the matter and energy into their accretion disks and spit it out completely digested into another dimension. I could go on but these thoughts flashed through my head while I was supposedly trying to relax. To make things worse she said that we should think of spreading ourselves out into a pool that was one molecule deep. I have a hard enough time keeping track of my socks after a workout – how the hell could I reintegrate my molecular structure with such an annoying background commentary.

Nick … velvet-headed, glib, so smooth that butter would not melt on any body parts – keeper of the front desk. Nick's job is to make everyone feel comfortable at the Y and he seems to have an unerring knack for doing just that. That alone really spurs me to poke him (verbally) like very crazy Canadians do to sleeping bears in the winter just to see if they can get a reaction. He can always make an irate customer calm down and he can divert any question in a way that makes the questioner question why they asked the question. He may be a bit distracted by the sheer number of crazies that he has to deal with but I am a little concerned about his mental health. This morning, he was telling me about himself and his sister and as this was happening he greeted a staff member and then related to her that his sister had just had a baby and he was really excited about being an uncle. He then returned to our conversation and all I could say was, "Whoa … your sister just had a baby and it slipped your mind to tell me while you were actually talking about your sister?" I strongly suspect that lurking under that calm exterior is a potentially very interesting serial murderer … maybe Nick Lector!

This morning (08/29/2016) I was at the gym at about 6:30am to work out before my workouts (don't even bother to ask). Nick, at the front desk, reached over and handed me a YMCA water bottle and bag and said, "These are yours".

My immediate response was, "No they are not, besides, they clash with my eyes."

"You won them! You won 2 of the four weeks of core challenges – side planks and leg lifts".

I smiled a little because I apparently beat out Sufiyan – a mythical 30-year-old handsome "beast". Wow! I then went to the locker room to get changed and AJ and James were there changing. AJ asked what I had in my hands and I mistakenly actually told him that they were prizes.

His response, so AJ, and so to the point. "So, you won a water bottle worth about $1.00 and an awful colored bag. What did you do for that?"

"32 minutes of side planks and 1004 leg lifts, one challenge per week of each". He just smiled and said nothing - that really drove in the knife. Clearly, I am the fittest, dumbest, 63-year-old in West LA who is currently without a woman. Holy crap on a cracker, without a word or even a moment of hesitation I went out to my truck and took a long sip of old vine zin – a necessary recalibration so-to-speak (it was about 6:45am).

The bottom line is that I really have to get a life that is not so clearly a joke!

The YMCA has a definite place on the inner-most spiral of the accretion disk. I feel that if I spend any more time there I will get sucked into the black hole but it seems that I am powerless to counteract the fascination I have with the cross-section of personalities and the panoply of mini-dramas.

CONCLUSION – THERE IS NONE!

OF COURSE, THERE IS NO CONCLUSION ... HOW COULD THERE BE?

The accretion disk continues to spin around the black hole from which it cannot escape. The black hole swallows energy and events with no heart and no remorse and spits them out to be reconstituted into another dimension. The notes and stories will continue for as long as there are events and people to populate and create them. Even when some of us eventually get sucked into the black hole there will be others to replace us – that is an irony of the universe itself – creating the very things it destroys.

The universe does not give a flying f**k about any of us but the reverse can also be true – we should not be too concerned about what the universe is doing because we can't do anything about it anyway. We can only affect our own small world, ourselves and the people around us – our own little accretion disks. That is really not so very bad when one picks up a glass of wine, other appropriate spirit or whatever is your fancy and lays back to enjoy the crazy shit that is always happening with us, within us, and without us.

Perspective is critically important – Roz would probably say that maybe the black hole isn't black at all to the people on the other side!

ACKNOWLEDGEMENTS

To the community of people at the Culver-Palms YMCA, Los Angeles, who tolerate my verbal wanderings and inspire me to work a bit harder if not be a bit more silently.

To my siblings for living far enough away that I have credible excuses for not dropping into the war zone.

Celeste Bryant for reading, editing and not running away screaming or trying to get me, or herself, into therapy.

Roz – because just thinking about you calms me down and makes the disk not nearly so formidable. Gotta Love You!

Cover Verso

The base image is from the credited source and is quoted directly below with one author insertion *[italicized in squared brackets]*. Cover graphics added by Duane R. Chartier.

VERSO COVER

"Some details about the APOD of 2010 December 7

This picture is a computer-generated image of the distortions caused by a spherically symmetric, uncharged (Schwarzschild) black hole. (Note: all the images of this page are under CC-BY-SA 3.0 license. In case you intend to reuse them, please credit my name and institution, i.e., Alain Riazuelo, IAP/UPMC/CNRS.)

This picture *[the original picture, NOT on the back cover and without the superimposed black hole]* is familiar to many amateur or professional astronomers. It is almost centered of the Large Magellanic Cloud. Above it one easily notices the southernmost part of the Milky Way with, from left to right, Alpha and Beta Centauri, the Southern Cross, and then the huge Argo Navis, now split into three constellations (from left to right, Carina, Vela and Puppis). At the right of the picture, the brightest spot is Sirius, from Canis Major. The second brightest star, close to the LMC is Canopus. The brightest star of the lower part of the picture is Achernar, at the edge of Eridanus."

Website: http://www2.iap.fr/users/riazuelo/bh/APOD.php
Image: http://www2.iap.fr/users/riazuelo/bh/IMG/public/BH_LMC_APOD.jpg

www.ingramcontent.com/pod-product-compliance
Lightning Source LLC
Chambersburg PA
CBHW041606220426
43666CB00001B/2